REAL STORIES

Book B

STUDENT NURSES SAVE TRUCK DRIVER

WILLIAMSBURG, Ky. — Three weeks ago, Paul Davis was given up for dead. Today, the 24-year-old truck driver is on the road to getting well:

...n one hand and my four-year-old boy in the other. First, I stop at the school, hand my boy to the teachers, and then rush to work. After work I run back to the school to pick up my boy and then run to the market. Then I run home to start cooking supper, and then it takes time to feed

He might not be except for the quick work of six Cumberland College student nurses. They were traveling a few minutes behind his truck and got to him soon after it crashed.

The student nurses were on the way back from a day of training at an Oak Ridge hospital. When they saw the accident, they jumped out of their car. They were told that Davis was already dead, but they wouldn't move on without seeing for themselves. With the help of three men, they lifted him out. He was bleeding badly. One girl, Sandy Robinson, found an ice cream stick on the ground. She wrapped some gauze around it and made an airway down his throat. Another student, Kathy Taylor, held his tongue down.

Then a third student, Sandy Brooks, found a towel. She pressed down

THE MYSTERY BOOK THAT SAVED A CHILD

How could a mystery book save a child's li...

Nurse Martha Mait... sat next to the hospi... bed of the dying child... nurse looked sadly at... 19-month-old girl. ... child had a strange ... ness. The best doctors ... the world were unable ... tell what her illness w...

Then the nurse retu... to the mystery book she... reading. The book was ... Pale Horse. It was wri... by Agatha Christie, ...

Globe Book Company, Inc.
New York/Chicago/Cleveland

A DAY IN THE LIFE OF A RUSSIAN RUNNER

Is that the way it is in all families?

Maria Shamshurina (SHAM SHU REE NUH) is a very fast runner. She has won many races put on by the factory in Russia where she works. She was asked how she was able to stay in such good shape. This was her answer:

"I'm in shape because of the way I spend my day. It begins at 5:30 in the morning. I jump out of bed to cook for my husband and iron the clothes. Then I

ew what was causing the aths. But one thing al-ys happened to the one o died. His or her hair ll out."

Nurse Maitland put down r book and looked at the ng child. She began to ink. The little girl had e same symptoms** as the ple who had been killed Agatha Christie's book: e had high blood pres-re *** She had trouble athing. She did not seem hear when someone spoke her. And, finally, her ir had started to fall .

Nurse Maitland hesi-ted. Then she made up her d and went to see the tor. Everything else been tried, so the se's idea was tested. was right. Somehow the ld had taken into her ly more than ten times safe amount of the son. Now the doctors

in one hand and my four-year-old boy in the other. First, I stop at the school, hand my boy to the teachers, and then rush to work. After work I run back to the school to pick up my boy and then run to the market. Then I run home to start cooking supper, and then it takes time to feed them and get them all to bed. Then I start doing the wash so I can iron in the morning.

"My husband is soft be-cause I have made life easy for him. He doesn't hurry to and from work, and I have the table set when he gets home. He eats, puts on the television, plops down and reads the newspaper. And that's why I'm in such good shape ... and my husband

real stories

book B

Milton Katz

Michael Chakeres   Murray Bromberg

ISBN: 0-87065-203-6

Acknowledgments for previously published materials appear on page 184 of this text.

Edited by David J. Sharp
Illustrations by Harry J. Schaare
Cover design by Lawrence Schaeffer
Text design by Edward Zytko

PRINTED IN THE UNITED STATES OF AMERICA
0 9 8 7 6 5 4 3 2 1

ABOUT THE AUTHORS

MILTON KATZ, the chairman of English at Thomas Jéfferson High School, Brooklyn, N.Y., has been a high school reading coordinator and a program writer for the Responsive Environment Center. He was the editor of *Moonlight Review,* a national teachers' literary magazine. Mr. Katz holds the degrees of B.A. from Brooklyn College and M.A. from New York University.

MICHAEL CHAKERES, an expert in the field of reading and reading curriculum development, is Assistant Principal of English at Susan Wagner High School, Staten Island, New York. He is a reading consultant in the High School Reading Program, Board of Education, City of New York. He holds a Secondary School Principal's license from New York State and has been laboratory supervisor and coordinator of the Responsive Environment Program.

MURRAY BROMBERG has taught English and been Chairman of English at Thomas Jefferson High School, Brooklyn, New York. He is past president of the High School Principals' Association of New York City. Mr. Bromberg has also taught at Hofstra University. Now principal of Andrew Jackson High School, Queens, New York, he is a contributing author of several books including Globe's *Our American Language, Biography for Youth, World-Wide Essays* and *Literature of Mystery: Four Representative Types.* He has published articles in *Shakespeare Quarterly* and other periodicals. Mr. Bromberg holds the degrees of B.A. from Brooklyn College and M.A. from Columbia University.

ABOUT THE BOOK

Real Stories, Book B, contains true-to-life stories adapted from newspapers and magazines. These stories show the human side of things and were chosen to entertain you and arouse your curiosity. There are stories about people in many different situations. Some are funny, and some are serious; some will make you think, and some will surprise you. There are stories about young people and old people, men and women. In other words, you will find a mixture in *Real Stories* as you might find in life.

These reports of real-life happenings will hold your interest, and more than that, they will help you to become a better reader. There are questions that help you understand what you read, and questions to help you know the meanings of some new words. Each selection in *Real Stories* teaches you how to learn new words and how to make better use of words you already know. In addition, you are invited to express yourself in writing or in class discussion on lively topics.

Ahead of you are worthwhile hours with stories of unusual events in the lives of ordinary, and not so ordinary, people. We know that you will enjoy the stories and lessons in *Real Stories, Book B.*

CONTENTS

1. ROUND AND ROUND

HAVE YOU EVER RIDDEN ON A ROLLER COASTER? A YOUNG MAN SPENT OVER FOUR DAYS ON ONE WITHOUT A STOP.

WHY DO YOU THINK HE DID IT?

NEW YORK, N.Y. (UPI)—After a few times around on a roller coaster, most people are glad to get off. The fast *speed shakes* up their insides. The *sharp* turns and quick drops leave them *dizzy*.

Last night, 19-year-old Richard Roderiguez did something that's very hard to believe. He finished almost 104 *hours* of roaring around the Cyclone * at Coney Island. Roderiguez set a new world *record* for hours of riding a roller coaster

---

* The Cyclone — a well-known roller coaster in Brooklyn, New York.

without a stop. The old record on another roller coaster was 101 hours.

Roderiguez went around 2,361 times! That's a record, too. The old record for trips around the Cyclone was 1,001.

The Cyclone has a 91-foot drop. It reaches speeds of up to 60 *miles* an hour. How was Roderiguez able to do it? He drives racing cars for a *hobby*. Maybe he's used to riding in fast machines.

"He would have gone on," said a friend, "but the people who ran the Cyclone got tired out."

There was a heavy rain just before Roderiguez finished. "Heavy *clothing* was put over Richard and he was roped into his seat," his friend said. "Would you believe he fell asleep and *slept* five hours?"

—MILWAUKEE JOURNAL

CHECK YOUR UNDERSTANDING

1. Richard Roderiguez rode the roller coaster for
   (A) 101 hours
   (B) 104 hours
   (C) 2,361 hours
2. He went around the Cyclone
   (A) 104 times
   (B) 1,001 times
   (C) 2,361 times
3. Roderiguez stopped riding the roller coaster because
   (A) he got tired
   (B) it started to rain heavily
   (C) the people who ran the Cyclone got tired

4. His hobby of driving racing cars may have helped Roderiguez break the record because he
  (A) was used to riding in fast machines
  (B) could drive the Cyclone himself
  (C) knew how to keep from getting tired

5. Which title tells most about the story?
  (A) Riding Around in the Rain
  (B) Roller Coaster Rider Breaks Record
  (C) The Cyclone at Coney Island

FIND THE MISSING WORD

In your notebook, complete the following sentences with words from the story. You may look back at the story.

  1. The fast speed on a roller coaster . . . . up their insides.
  2. The . . . . turns leave you dizzy.
  3. Roderiguez finished almost 104 . . . . of riding a roller coaster without a stop.
  4. Roderiguez set a new world . . . . for hours of riding a roller coaster without a stop.
  5. The Cyclone can go as fast as 60 . . . . an hour.

BY THE NUMBERS

You'll need to do a little arithmetic to find the right answers to these questions.

  1. 104 hours is closest to
  (A) 2 days
  (B) 4 days
  (C) 8 days

2. Roderiguez broke the old record for riding a roller coaster without a stop by
   - (A) 1 hour
   - (B) 3 hours
   - (C) 5 hours

3. Roderiguez broke the old record for rides around the Cyclone by
   - (A) 360 trips
   - (B) 1,360 trips
   - (C) 2,360 trips

4. A speed of 60 miles an hour means you are going
   - (A) 1 mile a minute
   - (B) 2 miles a minute
   - (C) 3 miles a minute

IMPROVING YOUR VOCABULARY

Choose the best word in Column B to complete each sentence in Column A. Use each word in Column B only once.

A	B
1. Jerry's . . . . is saving stamps.	(a) slept
2. I'm so tired, I feel as if I haven't . . . . for three days.	(b) speed
	(c) hobby
3. Wear heavy . . . . because it's going to be cold today.	(d) dizzy
	(e) clothing
4. The . . . . of this airplane is 500 miles an hour.	
5. If you spin around too many times, you can get	

4

SPELL IT RIGHT

Look at words carefully. Spelling a word can be easy when you find parts in the word you already know. Sometimes you will see a word that is made up of two little words. Such a word is called a *compound word*. The word *around* in this story is a compound word. It is made up of two words: *a* and *round*.

A. Write the two little words in each of these compound words found in the story. The first one is done for you.
   1. inside   *in side*
   2. something
   3. without
   4. maybe
   5. asleep

B. Write the one word in each pair which is spelled right. Don't look back.
   1. somthing, something
   2. maybe, mabe
   3. inside, insid
   4. assleep, asleep
   5. witout, without

C. Fill in the missing letter in each word.
   1. in . .ide
   2. witho . .t
   3. ma . . be
   4. som . .thing
   5. asle . .p

D. One of these five words is spelled wrong. Pick out that wrong word and spell it right.

   asleep   maybe   without   somthing   inside

EXPRESSING YOURSELF

1. Some people like to see their names in print as holders of world records. They swallow goldfish, they drink many pitchers of beer, or they dance for hundreds of hours. Tell of a record you would like to have.

2. What kind of person do you think Richard is? Would you want him as a friend? Why?

3. Go to your school or neighborhood library and ask to see *The Guinness Book of Records*. There you will be able to read about people who set records as strange as Richard Roderiguez's. Copy three records which you think are very interesting.

4. Tell about something unusual that you, or someone you know, does or has done.

WRITE NOW!

1. Imagine that your best friend wants to set a record for eating the most pizza pies within an hour. Write a paragraph describing the way he does it. Make us see the pies, his face, the crowd around him, etc.

2. (a) Write a paragraph telling why you think riding a roller coaster is fun.

(b) If you don't think it's fun, write a paragraph telling why.

2. A DAY IN THE LIFE OF A RUSSIAN RUNNER

THIS PERSON SAYS HER HUSBAND HAS IT EASY WHILE SHE DOES THE HARD WORK.

IS THAT THE WAY IT IS IN ALL FAMILIES?

Maria Shamshurina (SHAM SHU REE NUH) is a very fast runner. She has *won* many races put on by the *factory* in Russia where she works. She was asked how she was able to stay in such good *shape*. This was her answer:

"I'm in shape because of the way I *spend* my day. It begins at 5:30 in the morning. I jump out of bed to cook for my *husband* and *iron* the clothes. Then I wake up the family and get the children dressed and feed them and my husband. Then I have to start running to make it to work on time.

"I run with a large bag in one hand and my four-year-old boy in the other. First, I stop at the school, hand my boy to the teachers, and then *rush* to work. After work I run back to the school to pick up my boy and then run to the *market*. Then I run home to start cooking supper, and then it takes time to feed them and get them all to bed. Then I start doing the wash so I can iron in the morning.

"My husband is soft because I have made life easy for him. He *doesn't* hurry to and from work, and I have the table set when he gets home. He eats, puts on the television, plops down and reads the *newspaper*. And that's why I'm in such good shape . . . and my husband isn't."

—MIAMI HERALD

CHECK YOUR UNDERSTANDING

1. Maria Shamshurina is special because she
   (A) lives in the United States
   (B) thinks that men work harder than women
   (C) is a very fast runner
2. In the morning, Maria usually
   (A) irons the clothes
   (B) goes to the market
   (C) washes the clothes
3. After work, Maria usually
   (A) takes her boy to school
   (B) irons the clothes
   (C) cooks supper
4. Maria says that when her husband comes home, he
   (A) works around the house
   (B) puts on the television and reads a newspaper
   (C) eats supper and then goes out

5. Which title tells most about the story?

  (A) A Woman on the Go
  (B) Getting Up Early
  (C) Going to School

FIND THE MISSING WORD

In your notebook, complete the following sentences with words from the story. You may look back at the story.

  1. Maria works in a . . . .
  2. She was asked how she was able to stay in such good . . . .
  3. In the morning, she jumps out of bed to cook and to . . . . the clothes.
  4. After work, she runs back to the school and then runs to the . . . .
  5. My husband . . . . hurry to and from work.

WHAT'S THE REASON?

When you read, you sometimes have to be a good detective. You have to find out *why* things happen. See if you can find the right "why" to answer each of these questions.

1. Maria Shamshurina is in good shape because she
  (A) works in a factory
  (B) goes to exercise classes
  (C) runs so much every day
2. Maria gets up at 5:30 in the morning because
  (A) her children wake her
  (B) she has so much to do before she goes to work
  (C) she likes to get up early

3. Maria says her husband is soft because
  (A) she has made life easy for him
  (B) he doesn't go to work
  (C) he washes and irons clothes
4. Maria does the wash at night so she
  (A) will have something to do
  (B) can sleep in the morning
  (C) can iron in the morning

IMPROVING YOUR VOCABULARY

A. Choose the best word in Column B to complete each sentence in Column A. Use each word in Column B only once.

A	B
1. We read about the fire in the morning	(a) won
2. The school basketball team .... the game on Leo's basket in the last second of play.	(b) husband (c) rush (d) newspaper
3. You'll have to .... to get to work on time.	(e) spend
4. How are you going to .... your day?	
5. She told her .... to pick up the children at school.	

B. The ten new words in this story are:
  won   factory   shape   spend   husband
  iron   rush   market   doesn't   newspaper

Use each of these words once to complete the blank spaces in the little story that follows.

10

Maria's . . . . said he was getting
fat. He said he wouldn't . . . . his time
after supper watching TV and reading the
. . . . He said he would help Maria
with her work. He said that he wanted to be in
good . . . . too. He said Maria would
still cook and wash and . . . . the clothes
and buy food at the . . . . , but that he
would dress the children, take them to school
and get them ready for bed.
Maria's not sure she'll like this. She says
that she likes it that she has . . . . races
against other runners. If she . . . . hurry
to get to work at the . . . . and then
. . . . home, she may slow down and
not win anymore.

SPELL IT RIGHT

In the last lesson (p. 5), we learned about
compound words. Which of these words is a compound word: *begins* or *because?*
Some words are not compound words but have
in them a word part you already know. For example, the word *market* in this story has in it the
smaller word *mark*. As you learn to spell a word,
look to see if it has a smaller word in it. If it has,
it will help you to spell the bigger word.
A. Write the smaller word in each of these words
found in the story. The first one is done for you.

1. clothes   *cloth*
2. running
3. children
4. cooking
5. begins

B. Write the one word in each pair which is spelled right. Don't look back.
  1. children, chilren
  2. begins, beggins
  3. cooking, cooken
  4. clothz, clothes
  5. runing, running

C. Fill in the missing letter in each word.
  1. co . . king
  2. chil . . ren
  3. run . . ing
  4. clo . . hes
  5. b . . gins

D. One of these five words is spelled wrong. Pick out that word and spell it right.
  begins
  cooking
  clothes
  runing
  children

EXPRESSING YOURSELF

1. In what ways is Maria's life like the lives of other wives? In what ways is it different?
2. Who usually has a harder life—the wife, or the husband? Tell why you think so.
3. Are you in good shape? If you don't think so, tell what you would need to do to get in good shape.
4. Does it sound as though Maria enjoys her life? Would you like to lead a life like hers? Why, or why not?

WRITE NOW!

In order to write well, you must be able to write a paragraph well. The paragraph is the key to all good writing.

Try to remember these important paragraph rules:

1. A paragraph is a group of sentences written around one main idea.
2. The main idea is usually stated in a *topic sentence.*
3. The rest of the paragraph *proves* the main idea. (A well-done paragraph makes the reader see that the main idea is true. A poorly written paragraph leaves the reader not believing the truth of the main idea.)

Write a paragraph telling about Maria's day. A good topic sentence would be:

Maria has a lot to do during the day.

Before writing the rest of your paragraph, you first must take some time to think and plan. In your notebook, list five things Maria does during the day.

Now you are ready to write your paragraph. First, copy the topic sentence. Now, use one sentence for each of the five ideas you listed. You should then have a good six-sentence paragraph on Maria's day. Remember to look over what you wrote and correct any mistakes you may have made.

3. THE KIDS DON'T BOTHER CHARLIE

DO PEOPLE PICK ON YOU?
WHAT DO YOU DO ABOUT IT?

WOULD YOU WANT TO DO
WHAT CHARLIE STIVALA DID?

Charlie Stivala passed his black *belt test* in karate * this week. He said he wasn't *nervous,* even though he was fighting someone much bigger. He also had to break a four-*inch-thick* board with his *bare* hands and feet.

Is Charlie some strong six-footer? No. He's a 4-feet-2, 11-year-old sixth-grader. He is very, very

---

* Karate — a way of fighting, first used in China and Japan. The fighter hits by using hands, elbows, knees, and feet.

young to win a black belt. The black belt is given only to those who are the very best in karate.

Charlie has been *learning* karate from the time he was 7½ years old. He *practices* about an hour a day and takes *classes* two times a week. He has won prizes. "Not many kids this young stick it out this long," his teacher said.

Charlie started taking up karate because kids "kept *bothering* me and, after I would fight with them, they still kept bothering me. The kids don't bother me much anymore."

"I try to teach him to talk his way out of a fight," his father said. "He's doing the karate more for fun." But Charlie said he still gets into fights. The other day a bigger boy was bothering a friend of his, so Charlie helped his friend out. The 11-year-old said he doesn't always use karate when he fights "because I could hurt them a lot."

—NEWSDAY (LONG ISLAND, N.Y.)

CHECK YOUR UNDERSTANDING

1. To pass his black belt test in karate, Charlie Stivala had to
  (A) break a four-inch-thick board
  (B) be nervous
  (C) be more than 12 years old
2. How old is Charlie Stivala?
  (A) 6 years old
  (B) 7½ years old
  (C) 11 years old
3. Since Charlie started taking up karate, other kids bother him
  (A) less than they used to
  (B) as much as they used to
  (C) more than they used to

15

4. Charlie's father tries to teach him to
  (A) run away from fights
  (B) use karate when he fights
  (C) talk his way out of a fight
5. Which title tells most about the story?
  (A) Passing Tests
  (B) Fighting Bigger Boys
  (C) Eleven-Year-Old Black Belt

FIND THE MISSING WORD

In your notebook, complete the following sentences with words from the story. You may look back at the story.

  1. Charlie passed his black . . . . test in karate.
  2. He had to break a four- . . . . -thick board.
  3. He had to break the board with his . . . . hands and feet.
  4. Charlie has been . . . . karate from the time he was 7½ years old.
  5. He takes . . . . two times a week.

WHAT'S THE REASON?

When you read, you sometimes have to be a good detective. You have to find out *why* things happen. See if you can find the right "why" to answer each of these questions.

1. The kids don't bother Charlie much anymore because he
  (A) is much bigger than they are
  (B) talks his way out of fights
  (C) is so good at karate

2. Charlie is different from most boys his age because he is
   (A) a black belt in karate
   (B) 4-feet-2
   (C) in the sixth grade
3. Charlie is good at karate because he
   (A) is very strong
   (B) is young
   (C) practices every day
4. Charlie doesn't always use karate when he fights because
   (A) he doesn't know it well enough
   (B) he's afraid he will hurt the person he is fighting
   (C) it doesn't work well against bigger boys

IMPROVING YOUR VOCABULARY

A. Choose the best word in Column B to complete each sentence in Column A. Use each word in Column B only once.

A	**B**
1. The little girl was .... riding in the airplane alone.	(a) test
	(b) nervous
2. The football team ...... two or three hours every day.	(c) thick
	(d) practices
	(e) bothering
3. That book is so .... it will take me a year to finish it.	
4. The flies were .... Ron, so he went inside.	
5. Every time Ellen takes a .... she gets 100 percent.	

B. Write the letter before the word in Column B which is most nearly *opposite* to the word in Column A.

A	B
1. bare	(a) calm
2. learning	(b) thin
3. nervous	(c) covered
4. thick	(d) forgetting
5. bothering	(e) helping

SPELL IT RIGHT

In the last lesson, we learned to look for smaller words within bigger words. Which of these words has a smaller word in it: *bigger* or *break*?

Letters to remember in spelling are *a, e, i, o, u,* and sometimes *y*. These are the *vowels*. Just about every sound in every English word has a vowel.

Sometimes you find two vowels together. One of the vowels is sounded and the other is silent. The word *people* in the headline to this story has two vowels together: *e* and *o*. The *e* is sounded and the *o* is silent.

A. Copy each of these words. Underline the two vowels that are together. Then, draw a line through the vowel that is silent. The first one is done for you.

1. through   thrøugh
2. break
3. young
4. teach
5. friend

B. Write the word in each pair which is spelled right. Don't look back.
  1. teach, taech
  2. friend, freind
  3. yung, young
  4. thrugh, through
  5. brak, break
C. Fill in the missing letter in each word.
  1. yo . ng
  2. t . ach
  3. fr . end
  4. br . ak
  5. thr . ugh
D. One of these five words is spelled wrong. Pick out that wrong word and spell it right.

   teach   freind   young   break   through

EXPRESSING YOURSELF

1. Charlie studied and practiced every day for four years to become a karate black belt. If Charlie had spent that much time studying the piano, he might have become quite good at that, too. Do you think karate is a useful thing to learn? Why or why not?

2. Charlie's dream was to help himself through karate. He made his dream come true through practice and hard work. What do you dream of doing? How could you make your dream come true?

3. Tell about someone you know or read about who improved himself or herself through practice and hard work.

4. How is it possible for a boy Charlie's size and

age to break a four-inch-thick board with his bare hands and feet? Go to the library and see if you can learn more about karate. Write down three new facts you learn from your reading.

5. If you have studied karate, tell the class about it. If not, talk to someone in your school who has taken karate lessons. Ask him or her to tell you about it. Visit a karate school if there is one in your neighborhood. Report to your class on what you have learned.

WRITE NOW!

Write a paragraph using this as your topic sentence:

I would like to . . . .

Fill in the end of the sentence with something you'd like to do.

Plan before you write. In your plan, answer questions like, "*Why* would you like to?" "*How* did you become interested?" and "*What* will you do to make your wish come true?"

Remember to look over what you write and correct any mistakes you may have made. This is called *proofreading*.

4. THE FOOTBALL PLAYER

TRY TO IMAGINE PLAYING FOOTBALL WITH ONE LEG. "IT CAN'T BE DONE," YOU SAY.

HOW DID CARL JOSEPH PROVE THAT YOU ARE WRONG?

MADISON, Fla. (UPI) — His *coach* says that Carl Joseph does what he has to on the field. The 170-*pound* tackle * was *born* without a left leg. He's only in his second year of high school, but he has played in almost every game this year.

Carl has played football and basketball with his four brothers and five sisters for years. He believes he can do just about anything people with

* Tackle — a line position on a football team.

two legs can do. "The other players on the *team treat* me like everyone else and that's the way I want it," he said. "Sure, I'm proud of what I can do, but I don't want to make such a big deal out of it."

He wears an *artificial* leg off the playing field. He can't wear it on the field because of a state high school *rule*.

How does Carl do it? When he's on the line he *leans* into a teammate. Then, when play starts, he throws himself at the player on the other team lined up *against* him. "He's strong," his coach said. "You have no idea how strong he is."

Head Coach Lavon Bell said he *decided* to let Carl come out for the team after seeing him play basketball. "I played basketball with him all summer long. After that, I was sure he wasn't going to get hurt," Bell said. "At first, I'd take it pretty easy with him while we were playing, and he'd beat me pretty bad. I don't know anything anyone with two legs can do that he can't do."

—JACKSONVILLE STAR

CHECK YOUR UNDERSTANDING

1. Carl Joseph plays football with only one
- (A) arm
- (B) leg
- (C) eye

2. Carl feels
- (A) sad that he is not captain
- (B) proud of what he can do
- (C) angry with his team

3. On the field, Carl plays the position of
- (A) tackle
- (B) halfback
- (C) fullback

4. The coach let Carl come out for the team because he
- (A) felt sorry for Carl
- (B) beat Carl in basketball
- (C) was sure Carl wouldn't get hurt

5. Which title tells most about the story?
- (A) High School Football
- (B) Beating the Coach in Basketball
- (C) An Unusual Young Athlete

FIND THE MISSING WORD

In your notebook, complete the following sentences with words from the story. You may look back at the story.

1. His .... says that Carl does what he has to on the field.
2. Carl was .... without a left leg.
3. The other players .... him like everyone else.
4. On the line, he .... into a teammate.
5. He throws himself at the player lined up .... him.

FIRST THINGS FIRST

Arrange these events in the order in which they really happened.

1. Carl played in almost every game on his high school football team.
2. Carl played football and basketball with his brothers and sisters.
3. Coach Bell let Carl come out for the football team.

4. Carl played basketball with Coach Bell.

5. Carl was born without a left leg.

IMPROVING YOUR VOCABULARY

A. Choose the best word in Column B to complete each sentence in Column A. Use each word in Column B only once.

A	**B**
1. We . . . . to go to the party instead of to the movies.	(a) pound
	(b) team
	(c) artificial
2. There are five players on a basketball	(d) rule
	(e) decided
3. Shirley was on a diet and was very happy because she lost a	
4. The flower looks so real, you can't tell it's	
5. One . . . . that Juan follows is never to be late.	

SPELL IT RIGHT

In the last lesson, we learned that when two vowels come together, one of the vowels may be silent. Underline the two vowels together in the following word, and then draw a line through the silent vowel: *deal*.

Sometimes we make two or more words into one word by leaving out one or more letters. To show that letters have been left out, we use the apostrophe ('). For example, the word *he's* in this

story is one word made from the two words *he is.*
The apostrophe between the *e* and the *s* shows that
a letter (*i*) has been left out. Words made in this
way are called *contractions.*

A. Write the words that the following contractions
from the story stand for. The first one is done for
you.

1. I'd   *I would*
2. I'm
3. don't
4. can't
5. wasn't

B. Write the word in each pair which is spelled
right. Don't look back.

1. do'nt, don't
2. Id, I'd
3. was'nt, wasn't
4. I'm, Im
5. can't, ca'nt

C. Write the contraction for each pair of words.

1. was not
2. do not
3. I am
4. I would
5. can not

D. One of these five words is spelled wrong. Pick
out that wrong word and spell it right.

was'nt   don't   I'd   I'm   can't

EXPRESSING YOURSELF

1. Why is Carl pleased that his teammates treat him
like anyone else?
2. How would you feel if you had to play against

Carl? Would you "take it easy" not to hurt him? Why?

3. What do you think Carl's parents are like? Why?
4. Carl's coach says of him: "You have no idea how strong he is." What do you think makes Carl so strong?
5. What is your opinion of Coach Bell? Why? Would every coach have let Carl come out for the team? Why not?
6. Here are five people who overcame handicaps, just as Carl Joseph is doing: Franklin Roosevelt, Jose Feliciano, Glenn Cunningham, Ray Charles, Helen Keller. Use your library to find out about at least three of them. Try to add to this list.

WRITE NOW!

Write a paragraph using this as your topic sentence:

Carl Joseph is a person to be admired.

Plan before you write. List at least three ideas to back up the topic sentence.
Remember to proofread.

EXTRA: Write a paragraph about someone you know who has been able to do well even though there was something wrong with him or her.

5. "THE HOT WHEELS KID"

WHY WOULD 33 TRUCK DRIVERS GO OUT OF THEIR WAY TO SEE AN 11-YEAR-OLD BOY?

WHAT MADE JUSTIN KENNEDY SO SPECIAL?

CHILLICOTHE, Texas (AP) — Justin Kennedy is 11 years old and has been *crippled* from *birth*. But he's *known* as "The Hot Wheels Kid" to the truck drivers who talk with him over CB radio.*

---

* CB radio — a Citizens' Band radio. A person with a CB radio can speak to and listen to another person with such a radio from a distance of 3 to 20 miles. Many people have CB radios in automobiles and trucks.

It was a thrill for Justin when he met his *heroes* for the first time. Thirty-three truck drivers roared one after another into Chillicothe, a tiny *north* Texas farm town, blowing their horns as they *arrived*. They all parked near the Kennedy home.

"It was the biggest surprise of my life," said Justin. "I used to ask them if they'd come by some time if they ever had the time."

The friends brought a *gift*. They gave Justin a CB *base* station that will let "The Hot Wheels Kid" talk to truck drivers up to 15 miles away. Until then, he had been talking to them over a radio that "The Jockey" had let him *borrow*.

Justin was taken outside to ride in the big trucks. "It was pretty cool," he said.

The first ride was in a truck driven by "The Playboy" from Salt Lake City. Justin said he does not know the driver's real name, but the CB name is the only one he needs to know.

Then Justin was *lifted* into the truck of "602" —Willie Thorp of Dallas. When the 18-wheeler rolled back to his home, Justin saw that the base station had been set up for him and he was ready to go on the air.

Justin's mother watched happily and said, "All these years I've been Justin's mother. Now I'll be known as the mother of 'The Hot Wheels Kid.' "

—THE DENVER POST

CHECK YOUR UNDERSTANDING

1. Justin Kennedy's CB name is
  (A) "The Jockey"
  (B) "The Playboy"
  (C) "The Hot Wheels Kid"

2. When the truck drivers came into the town where Justin lives, Justin was
   (A) waiting for them
   (B) surprised
   (C) unhappy
3. The truck drivers gave Justin a gift of
   (A) a CB base station
   (B) a truck
   (C) 18 wheels
4. The truck drivers seem to be
   (A) kind
   (B) unfriendly
   (C) quiet
5. Which title tells most about the story?
   (A) Driving a Truck
   (B) A Surprise Visit and Gift
   (C) Talking Over a Borrowed Radio

FIND THE MISSING WORD

In your notebook, complete the following sentences with words from the story. You may look back at the story.

   1. Justin Kennedy has been .... from birth.
   2. He's .... as "The Hot Wheels Kid."
   3. Justin met his .... for the first time.
   4. Chillicothe is a tiny .... Texas farm town.
   5. They gave Justin a CB .... station.

FIRST THINGS FIRST

Arrange the events at the top of the next page in the order in which they really happened.

1. Justin met 33 truck drivers for the first time.
2. Justin was given a ride in Willie Thorp's truck.
3. Justin saw that the CB base station had been set up for him.
4. Justin talked to truck drivers over a radio borrowed from "The Jockey."
5. Justin got a ride in "The Playboy's" truck.

IMPROVING YOUR VOCABULARY

A. Choose the best word in Column B to complete each sentence in Column A. Use each word in Column B only once.

A	B
1. When we . . . . , the lights were out in the house and we thought no one was home.	(a) lifted (b) borrow (c) birth (d) gift (e) arrived
2. The . . . . of a baby is a time of joy.	
3. Luis was so strong, he . . . . . . the car up with his bare hands.	
4. Nancy went to Mrs. Jenkins to . . . . a cup of sugar.	
5. What . . . . would you like for your birthday?	

SPELL IT RIGHT

Review of Words from Lessons 1-5

There is one word spelled wrong in each line. Pick out that word and spell it right.

1. asleep, break, chilren, cooking
2. friend, clothes, can't, dont
3. inside, I'm, mabe, I'd
4. somthing, running, teach, through
5. without, yung, wasn't, begins

In the last lesson, we learned that contractions can be made of two or more words by leaving out one or more letters. A contraction used in this story was *they'd*. Write the two words from which *they'd* was made.

When *ed* is placed at the end of most words, it means that the action has taken place in the past. For example, the word *lifted* in this story means that the lifting was done in the past time. Without the *ed*, *lift* would mean that the action is being done right now, in the present.

A. Add *ed* to each of these words to change them from present time to past time.
1. roar
2. park
3. roll
4. watch
5. use (CLUE: the *e* is already there)

B. Write the word in each pair which is spelled right. Don't look back.
1. used, usd
2. roard, roared
3. rold, rolled
4. parked, parkt
5. watched, watchd

C. Fill in the missing letter in each word.
1. us . . d
2. park . . d
3. r . . ared

4. watc. .ed
5. rol. .ed

D. One of these five words is spelled wrong. Pick out the wrong word and spell it right.

rolled   usd   watched   parked   roared

EXPRESSING YOURSELF

1. Why do you think the truck drivers went to visit Justin?
2. Justin calls himself "The Hot Wheels Kid" when he uses his CB radio. Why do you think he picked that name?
3. Everyone with a CB radio has a name that he is known by. In this story, we read about "The Jockey," "The Playboy," and "602." What name would you choose for yourself if you had a CB radio? Why?
4. Tell of three ways in which someone with a CB radio at home or in his car could help other people.
5. Suppose you and a friend were talking to each other on your CB radios. Write down some of the things you might say to each other. Get up in front of the class and act out what you would talk about.

WRITE NOW!

1. Imagine you are Justin Kennedy. Write a letter to a friend telling what happened on the day the truck drivers came to see you, and how you felt that day.

2. Write a paragraph using this as your topic sentence:

Three things made Justin happy on this day.

Plan first by listing the three things. Then, use one sentence for each.

When you move from one sentence to the next, use words like *First, Second, Then, Next, Also,* etc.

Remember to proofread.

URSES
SAVE
TRUCK
DRIVER

MSBURG, Ky. ---
ks ago, Paul Davis
up for dead To-
24-year-old truck
s on the road to
ell.

ght not be except
quick work of six
nd College stu-

shape This was her answer:
"I'm in shape because of
the way I spend my day. It
begins at 5:30 in the morning. I jump out of bed to
cook for my husband and

A DAY IN THE LIFE OF A RUSSIAN

THE MYSTER BOOK THAT SA CHILD

Nurse Martha Maitland
sat next to the hospital
bed of the dying child. The
nurse looked sadly at the
19-month-old girl. The
child had a strange ill-
ness. The best doctors in
the world were unable to
tell what her illness was.

Then the nurse returned
to the mysterious book sh
read...

REVIEW OF LESSONS 1-5

FINDING THE MISSING WORD

The sentences below are followed by a list of *italicized* words. For each sentence, write the word that fits best in the blank. Use each word only once. (The number in parentheses tells you the number of the story in which the word was first used.)

1. Rosa was .... every time her sister was late in coming home.
2. We each gave a quarter to help buy a .... for our teacher.
3. Tommy's big brother got a job in an auto ....

4. On TV we saw a good program about the
.... of a baby.

5. Uncle David kept turning me around and
around until I became ....

6. Because she hopes to be a great skater, Ethel
.... for three hours a day.

7. Judge Diaz became an important person even
though he is badly ....

8. One .... we have to follow at our school
is that no one may smoke in the building.

9. Tina brought back beautiful apples from the
....

10. When the mail ...., I quickly tore open
the letter.

(a) *arrived* (5)	(f) *gift* (5)
(b) *birth* (5)	(g) *market* (2)
(c) *crippled* (5)	(h) *nervous* (3)
(d) *dizzy* (1)	(i) *practices* (3)
(e) *factory* (2)	(j) *rule* (4)

FINDING THE OPPOSITE

For each of the words in capitals, choose the
word on the right that is most nearly OPPOSITE.
(The number in parentheses tells you the number of
the story in which the word was first used.)

1. WON (2) (A) each (B) lost (C) first

2. SPEND (2) (A) save (B) buy (C) shop

3. BORROW (5) (A) lose (B) ask for (C) lend

4. SLEPT (1) (A) awoke (B) dozed (C) left

35

5. THICK (3)   (A) shake (B) thin (C) meat

6. NORTH (5)   (A) south (B) Alaska (C) snowy

7. BORN (4)   (A) raised (B) halted (C) died

8. ARTIFICIAL (4)   (A) real (B) leg (C) cane

9. LIFTED (5)   (A) took (B) put down (C) sent up

10. HUSBAND (2)   (A) family (B) father (C) wife

UNSCRAMBLING THE WORD

Each of the definitions below is followed by a scrambled word that fits the meaning. Unscramble the letters to find the word. (The number in parentheses tells you the number of the story in which the word was first used.)

1. something to do in your spare time (1)   YHBOB

2. the best that anyone has done (1)   COREDR

3. giving someone trouble (3)   ITHBOGERN

4. strong and brave people (5)   SEEROH

5. made up one's mind (4)   CEDEDID

6. hurry (2)   HURS

7. someone who tells players what to do (4)   OCACH

8. to press clothes (2)   INOR

9. to behave toward someone or thing (4)   RETAT

10. sixteen ounces (4)   DUNOP

FILL IN THE MISSING LETTERS

For each of the words below, write in the missing letters. (The number in parentheses tells you the number of the story in which the word was first used.)

1. s . . . . . p (1)   having a point or edge
2. b . . . e (3)   without any covering
3. a . . . . t (4)   next to
4. s . . . . . e (2)   state of health
5. b . . . . w (5)   take to pay back later
6. m . . . . . . t (2)   place where food is sold

6. BULLETPROOF VEST

HOW BIG A PART DOES LUCK PLAY IN LIFE?

WHAT WOULD HAVE HAPPENED TO DAVID SCHAEFER IF . . . ?

Terry Schaefer knew just what she wanted to get her husband. It was a gift. She wanted to buy him a bulletproof vest.*

It was not a bad idea. Her husband David was a police officer. Terry went to a little shop to buy

---

* Bulletproof vest — a piece of clothing, worn under a coat or jacket, that can stop bullets. The vest Terry Schaefer bought her husband weighed almost three pounds.

the vest. That was her second good idea. She looked the vests over and picked one out. She asked how much it was.

"They sell for $127.50," she was told.

Terry shook her head. It was just too much. "I'll pay little by little," she said, "and pick it up before Christmas."

Then the owner of the store told her, "Go ahead. Take it with you." He said, "You can pay me later. After all, I *trust* you. Why should I make the man wait for Christmas? The police are in *danger* all the time."

So David got his bulletproof vest. It was lucky he got it when he did. Not long after, he got a call on the *police* radio. A *robbery* was going on. He got there and chased the robber's car. He stopped it three blocks away. He *ordered* the robber out. The man came out with a *gun* in his hand. He fired at David's *stomach* from *three* feet away.

David was not even knocked off his feet. He *raised* his gun, fired at the man, and chased him down the street. Later, at a *hospital,* David was found to have a *bruise* the size of a baseball on his stomach.

"There's no question but that if I wasn't wearing the vest, Terry and the kids would be having Christmas dinner without me," David said.

—CHICAGO SUN-TIMES

CHECK YOUR UNDERSTANDING

1. Terry Schaefer bought a bulletproof vest for
   (A) herself
   (B) the owner of the store
   (C) her husband

2. After she went to the store, she
   (A) took the vest home with her
   (B) did not buy the vest
   (C) picked up the vest just before Christmas
3. When the robber fired his gun at him, David Schaefer was
   (A) not hit
   (B) wearing his bulletproof vest
   (C) wounded in the arm
4. When David got to the hospital it was found that he had a
   (A) bruise
   (B) head injury
   (C) cut hand
5. Which title tells most about the story?
   (A) A Lucky Gift
   (B) A Big Bruise
   (C) A Mean Store Owner

FIND THE MISSING WORD

In your notebook, complete the following sentences with words from the story. You may look back at the story.

   1. David got a call on the . . . . radio.
   2. He got a call on the radio that a . . . . was going on.
   3. The robber came out of the car with a . . . . . . in his hand.
   4. He fired at David from . . . . feet away.
   5. David was found to have a . . . . the size of a baseball on his stomach.

FIRST THINGS FIRST

Arrange these events in the order in which they really happened.

1. The robber fired his gun at David.
2. The owner of the store told Terry to take the vest home with her.
3. Terry gave her husband a bulletproof vest as a gift.
4. Terry wanted to buy her husband a gift.
5. David went to the hospital.

IMPROVING YOUR VOCABULARY

A. Choose the best word in Column B to complete each sentence in Column A. Use each word in Column B only once.

A	**B**
1. The policeman .... the robber to drop his gun.	(a) raised
2. The new girl in the class .... her hand to ask the teacher a question.	(b) ordered
	(c) trust
3. They rushed the sick child to the	(d) hospital
4. Walking down the dark street, Bob felt that he was in	(e) danger
5. It's a great feeling to know that your friends .... you.	

SPELL IT RIGHT

In the last lesson, we learned how to tell if action was taking place in the past time. Which of these shows action in the past: *wanted* or *sell*?

Some words have the same sounds, but have different spellings and meanings. These words are called *homonyms*. For example, the word *one* in the story has the same sound as the word *won*. Of course, *one* means the number 1, while *won* means that you came out the winner.

A. Here are some words in the story and their homonyms. They are used in sentences. Write the word in the parentheses that would make each sentence right. The first one is done for you.

1. I have a (new/knew) hat. (The right answer is *new*.)
2. Mary is going to (buy/by) a coat.
3. I'm going (to/too/two) the game.
4. Will you (wait/weight) for me?
5. Bob will meet you (there/their/they're).

B. Fill in the missing letter of the word in the parentheses.

1. I (. new) Jack many years ago.
2. Ken's father will (b . y) a new car.
3. Paul will be there and Nora will be there (t . o).
4. (Wa . t) here for me.
5. I'll see you (ther .).

C. One of these five words is spelled wrong. Pick out the wrong word and spell it right.

> too   wat   there   buy   knew

EXPRESSING YOURSELF

1. If Terry hadn't thought of buying the vest, and if the owner of the store hadn't trusted her for the money, David would have been killed. Was it luck that kept him alive? Explain.
2. Think of someone you like. What would be a good gift to buy for that person? Why?
3. What gift would you like someone to buy for you? Why?
4. A police officer has a dangerous job. Name three other jobs that are dangerous. Would you want to work at a job that was dangerous? Why, or why not?
5. The storekeeper showed kindness. Tell about some kind thing done for you by another person.

WRITE NOW!

Write a paragraph using either of these topic sentences:

Luck was with me that day.
Luck was against me that day.

If you need to write more than one paragraph in order to tell your story, do so.

7. A 73-YEAR-OLD HIGH DIVER

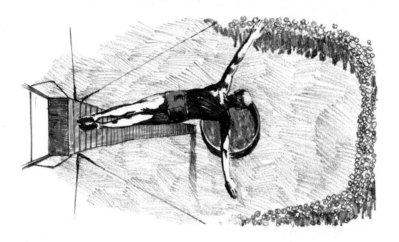

SOME PEOPLE SEEM OLD AT 40 WHILE OTHERS ARE YOUNG AT 80.

WHICH KIND IS HENRI LAMOTHE?

LOS ANGELES, Calif. — Henri LaMothe used to dive off a 40-foot *platform* into four feet of water.

No more. Now he jumps off a 40-foot platform into 12 inches of water.

So far, Henri has made more than 2,000 dives all over the world. When he hits the water, his *body* is falling at 35 miles an hour. What kind of life is this for an old man of 73, anyway?

"It's always been my life," he answers. "I started diving when I was six years old. I was a dancer, too. Even when dancing, I would dive like a plane and land on my stomach on the dance floor. Times were bad and work wasn't easy to find. That's when I started diving into the water for a living."

Henri doesn't dive head first. He belly flops.* "I use my stomach like a karate *chop.* Divers *usually* break the water with their hands as they *enter.* I use my stomach. If I landed any other way, it would *split* me open."

The other day, on his seventy-third birthday, he was getting ready for another dive. It was at a Los Angeles show. He looked as if he had borrowed the body of a much younger man. His hands held on to the *wires* behind him. He rocked back and forth on his feet.

Three minutes passed. At one point, he seemed ready, then shook his head. *Finally,* after almost four minutes, Henri threw himself into the air. His arms and legs were out, his eyes straight ahead. He never looks at the water as he dives.

When he plopped, the water splashed about 30 feet. His dive took 1¼ seconds. For Henri, it was a *perfect* belly flop, because he walked away from the landing.

—LOS ANGELES TIMES

* Belly flop — a dive in which the diver enters the water stomach first.

CHECK YOUR UNDERSTANDING

1. Henri LaMothe now dives off a 40-foot platform into

(A) 4 feet of water
(B) 12 inches of water
(C) 30 inches of water

2. Henri LaMothe first started diving when he was
   (A) three years old
   (B) six years old
   (C) nine years old

3. When Henri dives, he
   (A) uses his stomach like a karate chop
   (B) breaks the water with his hands
   (C) looks at the water as he dives

4. On Henri's seventy-third birthday, he
   (A) went to see a show
   (B) watched a younger man dive
   (C) was in Los Angeles, diving in a show

5. Which title tells most about the story?
   (A) An Old but Great Diver
   (B) Happy Birthday
   (C) Diving for Fun

FIND THE MISSING WORD

In your notebook, complete the following sentences with words from the story. You may look back at the story.

1. Henri LaMothe jumps off a 40-foot . . . .
2. When he hits the water, his . . . . is falling at 35 miles an hour.
3. He uses his stomach like a karate . . . .
4. His hands held on to the . . . . behind him.
5. It was a . . . . belly flop, because he walked away from the landing.

46

WHAT'S THE REASON?

When you read, you sometimes have to be a good detective. You have to find out *why* things happen. See if you can find the right "why" to answer each of these questions.

1. Henri now dives into 12 inches of water instead of 4 feet of water because it's
   (A) easier
   (B) more exciting for the people watching
   (C) a way to save water

2. Henri started diving for a living because
   (A) he was tired of dancing
   (B) it was easier than swimming
   (C) other work wasn't easy to find

3. Henri belly flops when he dives because
   (A) it looks exciting
   (B) the water isn't deep enough for him to safely break the water with his hands
   (C) that is the way he first learned to dive

4. Henri probably took almost four minutes before he did his dive because he
   (A) wanted to be ready to make a perfect dive
   (B) was afraid to jump
   (C) is an old man

5. Henri thought his dive was a perfect belly flop because
   (A) he did not get hurt
   (B) no one had ever made a better dive
   (C) he broke the water with his hands first

IMPROVING YOUR VOCABULARY

A. Choose the best word in Column B to complete each sentence in Column A. Use each word in Column B only once.

A	**B**
1. We couldn't wait to change into our bathing suits and .... into the water.	(a) split
	(b) usually
	(c) finally
2. Paul used an ax to .... the wood.	(d) dive
	(e) enter
3. After four tries, Maria ..... passed her driving test.	
4. Little Willy was afraid to .... the dark house alone.	
5. I'm surprised Ed isn't here yet since he's .... on time.	

SPELL IT RIGHT

In the last lesson, we learned about homonyms —words which sound alike, but have different spellings and meanings. Which of these two words from the story has a homonym: *dive* or *four*?

We learned that the vowel letters are *a, e, i, o, u,* and sometimes *y.* All the other letters are called *consonants.*

Sometimes, two or three consonants come together at the start of a word. When they do, they most likely make a *blend.* S is a letter that often blends with other consonants. For example, the word *split* in the story begins with a three-consonant blend: *spl.*

48

A. Copy each of these words. Then underline the letters at the start of the word that form a consonant blend beginning with *s*. The first one is done for you.
1. stomach   <u>st</u>omach
2. started
3. shook
4. straight
5. splashed

B. Write the word in each pair which is spelled right. Don't look back.
1. shook, shoock
2. splashd, splashed
3. stumach, stomach
4. started, startted
5. straight, strate

C. Fill in the missing letter in each word.
1. s . . ook
2. s . . omach
3. st . . aight
4. s . . arted
5. sp . . ashed

D. One of these five words is spelled wrong. Pick out the wrong word and spell it right.

    splashed   straigt   shook   stomach   started

EXPRESSING YOURSELF

1. How much do you think Henri earns for each dive? How much would you want to get paid for diving 40 feet into water 12 inches deep? Since Henri already has made more than 2,000 safe dives, do you think this is an easy trick? Why?
2. It has been said that people go to see Henri La-Mothe and others like him because they hope

that something will go wrong. Tell why you think this is true or not.

3. At what age do you think a person is old? Are young people happier than old people? Why?
4. What thoughts do you think were going through Henri's mind as he got ready to make his dive in Los Angeles?

WRITE NOW!

Write a paragraph using this topic sentence:

There is a right way and a wrong way to dive.

You may, if you wish, use another word or words in place of *dive*. (For example, *dribble a basketball; bake a cake; study; bring up a child; throw a football; drive a car*)

EXTRA: Write a paragraph or two about *one* of these topics: (Make up your own topic sentence.)

My Grandfather Is Full of Life
My Grandmother Is Full of Life
My High Dive
Taking Chances

8. DUMB BANK ROBBER

WHAT MADE ONE PERSON WISH THAT HE HAD LEARNED TO SPELL?

HOW WAS BAD SPELLING THIS PERSON'S DOWNFALL?

IF U CN RD THS, U CN MK GUD $ ROBING BNKS.

You can, that is, if the teller you hand your *note* to, can read it.

If she can't, you're in the same kind of trouble Tom Smith found himself in. He handed a Brooklyn bank teller a badly *written* stickup note. She pushed it back at him.

"I don't *understand* you," the teller told him. "You'll have to make it out again."

Smith got nervous. He put a finger on his lips to shush the teller. Then he turned around, walked back, and pulled out another bank *slip*.

Before he could write, "This is a robbery," *silent alarms* were ringing. A strong *customer* who had been told what had happened *wrestled* Smith to the ground.

"He was dopey, that I know," the teller said later. "He was very *stupid* and I think that's why I was so brave, because he just *appeared* very stupid."

As the police took him away, Smith must have been talking to himself. "If only I had learned to spell in school. . . . If only I had learned to spell in school. . . ."

—NEW YORK DAILY NEWS

CHECK YOUR UNDERSTANDING

1. Some words are spelled wrong in this story
   (A) because the writer of the story is a poor speller
   (B) to show that Tom Smith was a poor speller
   (C) because the teller was a poor speller
2. When the teller gave Smith back his note, he got
   (A) nervous
   (B) angry
   (C) happy
3. The strong customer wrestled Smith to the ground because he
   (A) was angry with Smith
   (B) felt like wrestling
   (C) found out Smith was trying to rob the bank

4. The teller thought that Smith was
   - (A) brave
   - (B) stupid
   - (C) strong
5. Which title tells most about the story?
   - (A) Bad Speller Gets in Trouble
   - (B) Wrestling in a Bank
   - (C) How to Rob a Bank

FIND THE MISSING WORD

In your notebook, complete the following sentences with words from the story. You may look back at the story.

1. Smith handed the teller a badly . . . . stickup note.
2. He turned around, walked back, and pulled out another bank . . . .
3. Silent . . . . were ringing.
4. A strong customer . . . . Smith to the ground.
5. The teller said, "He was very . . . . and I think that's why I was so brave. . . ."

FIRST THINGS FIRST

Arrange these events in the order in which they really happened.

1. The police took Smith away.
2. Smith handed the teller a badly written stickup note.
3. Smith walked back and took out another bank slip.

4. A customer wrestled Smith to the ground.

5. The teller told Smith to make out another note.

IMPROVING YOUR VOCABULARY

Choose the best word in Column B to complete each sentence in Column A. Use each word in Column B only once.

A	**B**

1. When everyone became .... I knew the teacher I had been making fun of was in the room.

(a) note
(b) appeared
(c) silent
(d) understand
(e) customer

2. Write a .... to your aunt thanking her for the beautiful present she gave you.

3. The .... asked the baker for bread and cake.

4. "I can't .... why you don't do better in school," her mother told Ann.

5. We were happy when George .... because we thought he had gotten lost.

SPELL IT RIGHT

Now that you saw what happened to Tom Smith because he couldn't spell, aren't you glad you are learning to spell and write?

In the last lesson, we learned that *s* sometimes comes together with one or two other consonants to form a blend at the start of a word. Which of these words begins with an *s* blend: *slip* or *silent*?

Just as *s* often begins a blend, *r* is often the second letter in a blend. Many words begin with *br, cr, dr, fr, gr, pr,* and *tr*. (*Wr* is also often used, though the *w* is silent.) For example, the word *dry* begins with a blend of which *r* is the second letter.

A. Copy each of these words. Then underline the letters at the start of the word that form a consonant blend with *r* as the second letter. The first one is done for you.
1. trouble   <u>tr</u>ouble
2. ground
3. brave
4. tried
5. write (not exactly a blend)

B. Write the word in each pair which is spelled right. Don't look back.
1. rite, write
2. brave, brav
3. trouble, troubel
4. ground, geround
5. tryed, tried

C. Fill in the missing letter in each word.
1. brav . .
2. w . ite
3. g . ound
4. tr . ed
5. tr . uble

D. One of these five words is spelled wrong. Pick out the wrong word and spell it right.

    tryed   trouble   write   brave   ground

1. A policeman said, "If Tom Smith knew how to spell, he wouldn't be holding up banks." What did he mean by that?
2. What should a teller do when someone tries to rob the bank? Should others act the way this teller did?
3. The teller said she felt brave because the robber was stupid. Why did she think he was stupid? Do you agree with her?
4. Although you don't know Tom Smith, make up a short life story about him. You might tell about his family, his schooling, his friends, etc.

WRITE NOW!

Begin a paragraph with the following words, and then finish it in your own words:

Sometimes I use my head, and sometimes I don't. Once. . . .

Your last sentence for this paragraph might be either: *That was one time I used my head.*

or

That was one time I didn't use my head.

EXTRA: Imagine you are the bank teller writing this paragraph. Finish this in "her" words:

Sometimes I use my head, and sometimes I don't. Once, while I was working in the bank, a young man came in and handed me a stickup note.

9. THE BITER

SOME PEOPLE WITH BAD TEMPERS DO AND SAY THINGS THEY'RE SORRY ABOUT LATER.

WOULD YOU WRITE TO A NEWSPAPER "ADVICE" COLUMN?

DEAR ANN LANDERS: My boyfriend is a sweet guy, but now and then I see signs of a terrible *temper.*

One night last week we were horsing around on the floor. I got a toe-hold * on him. I learned it

---

* Toe-hold — a wrestling hold where one wrestler twists the foot of the other wrestler.

from watching wrestling on TV. I think he went a little *crazy*, Ann. The guy bit me on the hand. I don't mean just a little bite. I mean a real bite that *broke* the *skin*. When I saw the *blood*, I nearly *fainted*.

Buzzy said he was sorry and that he'd lost his head. He said he'd never do such a thing again. I said I'd *forgive* him this time.

The next day my mother saw the bite and asked what happened. I was going to say that my dog Tuffy had done it. But I had to tell her the *truth*. My mother was very unhappy. She said a *human* bite can be very *dangerous*.

Is this true? So for I am O.K. Please tell me if Mom is right. *Nipped by Nick*
—WASHINGTON POST

CHECK YOUR UNDERSTANDING

1. The letter writer signs herself *Nipped by Nick*. She says that her boyfriend
   (A) has a sweet temper
   (B) is a sweet guy
   (C) doesn't like her
2. After *Nipped by Nick* got a toe-hold on Buzzy, he
   (A) hit her
   (B) fainted
   (C) bit her on the hand
3. After Buzzy said he was sorry, *Nipped by Nick* said
   (A) she'd forgive him
   (B) she never wanted so see him again
   (C) she was going to tell her mother
4. When her mother saw the bite, *Nipped by Nick* told her that

58

(A) her dog Tuffy had done it
(B) she did it herself
(C) her boyfriend had done it
5. Which title tells most about the story?
(A) Lying to Mother
(B) Wrestling on TV
(C) Trouble Over a Temper

FIND THE MISSING WORD

In your notebook, complete the following sentences with words from the story. You may look back at the story.

1. I see signs in Buzzy of a terrible . . . .
2. I think he went a little . . . ., Ann.
3. It was a real bite that broke the . . . .
4. When I saw the . . . ., I nearly fainted.
5. My mother said a . . . . bite can be very dangerous.

WHAT'S THE REASON?

When you read, you sometimes have to be a good detective. You have to find out *why* things happen. See if you can find the right "why" to answer each of these questions.

1. Buzzy bit *Nipped by Nick* because
   (A) he was watching wrestling on TV
   (B) she asked him to
   (C) he lost his temper
2. *Nipped by Nick* almost fainted because
   (A) she saw blood on her hand
   (B) she thought she had hurt Buzzy
   (C) of the toe-hold

3. *Nipped by Nick* told her mother the truth because
   (A) Buzzy told her to
   (B) she couldn't lie to her mother
   (C) Tuffy had bitten her
4. *Nipped by Nick*'s mother was unhappy because
   (A) Tuffy had bitten *Nipped by Nick*
   (B) *Nipped by Nick* had told a lie
   (C) she thought that a human bite could be dangerous
5. *Nipped by Nick* wrote to Ann to ask her if
   (A) a human bite is dangerous
   (B) she should still go out with Buzzy
   (C) she should run away from home

IMPROVING YOUR VOCABULARY

Choose the best word in Column B to complete each sentence in Column A. Use each word in Column B only once.

A	B
1. The baseball .... the window in Mr. Lee's living room.	(a) truth
	(b) broke
	(c) fainted
2. Rosa .... when she heard the bad news about her brother.	(d) dangerous
	(e) forgive
3. I couldn't tell whether or not Bob was telling the	
4. Leon asked Nancy to .... him for forgetting their date.	
5. It is .... to cross the street against the light.	

60

Review of Words from Lessons 1-8

A. Choose the word in Column B that is the best example of the rule or word in Column A.

A	B
1. compound word	(a) buy/by
2. contraction	(b) something
3. past time	(c) isn't
4. homonym	(d) start
5. consonant blend at the beginning of a word	(e) watched

B. There is one word spelled wrong in each line. Pick out that word and spell it right.

1. brak, asleep, watched, wait
2. children, cooking, buy, stumick
3. without, young, brave, straght
4. trubel, ground, wasn't, begins
5. freind, clothes, knew, parked
6. used, writ, I'm, maybe
7. don't, roared, cant, there
8. tryed, I'd, something, rolled
9. started, shook, insid, running
10. teach, thrugh, splashed, too

1. Why would someone write to Ann Landers or other "advice" columns? If you wanted the answer to a question, where would you go?
2. Why was the girl afraid to tell her mother the truth? How do you think her mother felt about Buzzy?

3. Should the girl have forgiven her boyfriend? Why? If she had not gotten him in a toe-hold, maybe he would not have bitten her. Was it all her fault? Explain.

4. Here is Ann Landers's answer to the letter:

Dear Nipped:
Yes, she is right. You were lucky. Every human mouth is loaded with bacteria. You could have gotten a bad infection.

If that clown ever bites you again, wash the wound with soap and water, see a doctor right away, and send Buzzy for a long walk on a short dock.

Would your advice to the girl be the same as Ann's? How would it be different?

WRITE NOW!

Write a paragraph telling about a time you lost or held your temper. Tell whether or not you think you did the right thing.

10. HERO FORGOT TO TELL MOM

WHAT IS YOUR IDEA OF A "HERO"?

CAN AN 11-YEAR-OLD BE A HERO?

LANSING, Mich. (UPI) — John Ryerse is an 11-year-old school *safety guard*. He is a hero. He got a *special award* for keeping four-and five-year-old children from getting hurt. Still, he *forgot* to tell his mother about what he did.

On the day John became a hero, many children were walking across a foot bridge. They were going to school. A *highway* crowded with cars ran under the bridge. Nearby, some men were working with a *huge* crane.* By *accident,* the crane *struck* the bridge and *tore* the bottom. Part of the bridge fell onto the highway. Six boys, from 8 to 11 years old, had broken legs and arms from the accident.

* Crane — a machine with a swinging arm used to lift heavy loads.

63

John was on guard on one end of the bridge. A number of children were in the middle of the bridge when part of it went down. John ran to the children, pulling them with him, then helping them off the bridge. He then blocked the way so that no other children could get in there until policemen came and blocked it off.

His mother said she first knew of the accident when the school called to tell her they were giving John a special safety award. "I didn't even know about it. He didn't tell me himself," she said.

—MIAMI HERALD

CHECK YOUR UNDERSTANDING

1. John Ryerse is a hero because he
   (A) is 11 years old
   (B) is a school safety guard
   (C) kept young children from getting hurt
2. The bridge the children were walking on was over a
   (A) highway
   (B) river
   (C) train track
3. The bottom of the bridge was torn by
   (A) cars
   (B) a crane
   (C) six boys
4. When John's mother heard about the accident she was
   (A) surprised
   (B) sad
   (C) angry
5. Which title tells most about the story?
   (A) School Safety Guards
   (B) Eleven-Year-Old Saves Younger Children
   (C) Mothers and Sons

FIND THE MISSING WORD

In your notebook, complete the following sentences with words from the story. You may look back at the story.

1. John Ryerse is a school .... guard.
2. He will get a special .... for keeping some children from getting hurt.
3. The crane .... the bridge.
4. A .... crowded with cars ran under the bridge.
5. By accident, the crane .... the bottom of the bridge.

FIRST THINGS FIRST

Arrange these events in the order in which they really happened.

1. A part of the bridge fell onto the highway.
2. John's mother found out he was going to get a special award.
3. John pulled some children away and helped them off the bridge.
4. A crane struck the bridge and tore the bottom.
5. The children were walking across a bridge on their way to school.

IMPROVING YOUR VOCABULARY

At the top of the next page choose the best word in Column B to complete each sentence in Column A. Use each word in Column B only once.

	A	**B**
1.	Rita . . . . it was Saturday and went to school.	(a) special
2.	Bill wants to get a job as a . . . . in a bank.	(b) accident
		(c) guard
3.	Larry weighs only 160 pounds and had to play on the line against a . . . . 250-pounder.	(d) huge
		(e) forgot
4.	So many people want to see that movie, there is going to be a . . . . 4 o'clock show.	
5.	Did anyone see how the . . . . happened at the street corner?	

SPELL IT RIGHT

The ending *ing* is often found at the end of a word that shows action. It means that the action is continuing, that it is still going on. For example, the word *giving* in the story brings across the idea of an action, *give,* still going on.

A. Copy each of these words. Then underline the letters *ing* at the end of each word. The first one is done for you.

1. walking   walk<u>ing</u>
2. working
3. pulling
4. going
5. helping

B. Write the word in each pair which is spelled right. Don't look back.

1. going, goeing
2. working, worken

66

3. helpin, helping
4. walking, wawking
5. pulling, puling

C. Fill in the missing letter in each word
1. he . . ping
2. pul . ing
3. goin . .
4. wo . king
5. walkin . .

D. One of these five words is spelled wrong. Pick out the wrong word and spell it right.

going   walking   puling   helping   working

EXPRESSING YOURSELF

1. Why didn't John Ryerse rush home to tell his mother about the great work he did in saving the younger children? What does that tell you about John? If you had saved people's lives, would you want everyone to know about it? Why?

2. Suppose John was not doing well in school. Should his teachers give him extra credit because he was a hero? Why or why not?

3. Make believe that you are the brother or sister of one of the children who was saved by John. Write a letter thanking him for his help.

WRITE NOW!

What is your idea of a hero? Someone who saves lives? Wins football games? Kills the enemy in a war? Makes a lot of money? Becomes the leader of a country? Something else?

Write a paragraph telling *your* idea of a hero.

Begin by writing your own topic sentence. Remember: the topic sentence gives the main idea of the paragraph.

A DAY IN THE LIFE

REVIEW OF LESSONS 6-10

FINDING THE MISSING WORD

The sentences below are followed by a list of *italicized* words. For each sentence, write the word that fits best in the blank. Use each word only once. (The number in parentheses tells you the number of the story in which the word was first used.)

1. Jose got an .... for bowling a perfect game.
2. .... beings are smarter than animals because they can think.
3. The bank .... happened in the morning when two men held up the guard.
4. Keep your .... clean by taking a shower every day.
5. Maria was a good .... who shopped at the store every day.

68

6. Have you . . . . a letter to your boyfriend?

7. The doctor . . . . the nurse to check the bruise on the boy's leg.

8. She used . . . . to hold up the pictures.

9. We worked all day, and . . . . it was time to quit.

10. A special . . . . switch will shut off the power in the factory.

    (a) *ordered* (6)   (f) *customer* (8)
    (b) *robbery* (6)   (g) *skin* (9)
    (c) *finally* (7)   (h) *human* (9)
    (d) *wires* (7)   (i) *safety* (10)
    (e) *written* (8)   (j) *award* (10)

FINDING THE OPPOSITE

For each of the words in capitals, choose the word on the right that is most nearly OPPOSITE. (The number in parentheses tells you the number of the story in which the word was first used.)

1. DANGER (6)   (A) calm (B) speed (C) safety

2. ENTER (7)   (A) leave (B) raise (C) care

3. FORGOT (10)   (A) took (B) remembered (C) missed

4. FORGIVE (9)   (A) blame (B) receive (C) hold

5. HUGE (10)   (A) tiny (B) round (C) straight

6. PERFECT (7)   (A) checked (B) correct (C) spoiled

7. RAISED (6)   (A) lifted (B) lowered (C) begun

8. SILENT(8)   (A) loud (B) angry (C) hard

9. STUPID (8)   (A) sad (B) smart (C) ill

10. TRUTH (9)   (A) love (B) hate (C) lie

UNSCRAMBLING THE WORD

Each of the definitions below is followed by a scrambled word that fits the meaning. Unscramble the letters to find the word. (The number in parentheses tells you the number of the story in which the word was first used.)

1. an important part of the body which receives food after you eat it (6)   CHOMAST

2. a special place for very sick people (6)   SHOALPIT

3. to cut meat into small pieces (7)   POCH

4. a raised even floor (7)   FLATMORP

5. threw or forced someone to the ground (8)   WELDREST

6. a little piece of paper (8)   LIPS

7. not having a healthy mind (9)   ZARCY

8. forced apart (9)   KROBE

9. a person who is on watch (10)   DUGAR

10. a main road (10)   WHAYHIG

70

FINDING THE RIGHT MEANING

Match each word in Column A to the best meaning in Column B. (The number in parentheses tells you the number of the story in which the word was first used.)

A	**B**

1. ACCIDENT (10)   (A) an event not planned (B) a place where it hurts (C) a minute of time

2. ALARMS (8)   (A) parts of the body (B) signals that warn (C) loud noise

3. APPEARED (8)   (A) was seen (B) was heard (C) was touched

4. BRUISE (6)   (A) warm drink (B) punch a bag (C) hurt on the body

5. DANGEROUS (9)   (A) unsafe (B) unkind (C) unfriendly

6. FAINTED (9)   (A) fooled around (B) fell as if dead (C) woke up

7. SPECIAL (10)   (A) put together (B) take away (C) set apart

8. SPLIT (7)   (A) tie together (B) cook outside (C) cut from end to end

9. TRUST (6)   (A) piece of bread (B) believe in (C) hate a lot

10. USUALLY (7)   (A) never (B) often (C) always

71

11. CIVIL WAR HEROINE

SOME PEOPLE ARE HONORED ONLY AFTER THEY ARE DEAD.

WHY DID IT TAKE 100 YEARS FOR MARY ELIZABETH BOWSER TO BE HONORED?

It took over 100 years for Mary Elizabeth Bowser to *receive* the *honor* that was coming to her. *Yet,* this unknown black woman played a part in the winning of the Civil War.

Mary Elizabeth Bowser was a *spy* for the North. She worked in the home of Jefferson Davis, the *President* of the South. She could not read or write. Still, she was able to remember *reports* she came across while working in the Davis home. She would then pass the reports along at secret *meetings* with another woman spy. The woman would then send the reports north to General Grant.

Mary's life was in *danger* every day. Yet, there is no record that she had ever been honored for her brave and important work. This wrong of *history* has now been made right, over 100 years later. She has finally been *recognized* for what she was—a true *heroine* of the Civil War.

CHECK YOUR UNDERSTANDING

1. Mary Elizabeth Bowser was a spy who
   (A) remembered reports found in the home of Jefferson Davis
   (B) took reports north to General Grant
   (C) wrote her reports at secret meetings
2. Mary Elizabeth Bowser was probably known to General Grant as
   (A) the person who sent him reports
   (B) a friend he often visited
   (C) a loyal member of the Jefferson Davis family
3. When was Mary Elizabeth Bowser honored?
   (A) Before the Civil War
   (B) After the Civil War
   (C) While the Civil War was being fought

4. Mary Elizabeth Bowser was a heroine because she
   (A) did brave and important work
   (B) worked for Jefferson Davis
   (C) did not want to be recognized
5. Which title tells most about the story?
   (A) One Hundred Years of the Civil War
   (B) Jefferson Davis Loses a Spy
   (C) How a Black Woman Helped the North

FIND THE MISSING WORD

In your notebook, complete the following sentences with words from the story. You may look back at the story.

1. It took over 100 years for Mary Elizabeth Bowser to .... the honor that was coming to her.
2. She worked for Jefferson Davis, the ...... of the South.
3. She would pass the reports along at secret ....
4. Mary Elizabeth Bowser was a .... for the North.
5. Mary's life was in .... every day.

FIRST THINGS FIRST

Arrange these events in the order in which they really happened to Mary Elizabeth Bowser.

1. She remembered reports she came across.
2. She was finally recognized as a true heroine.
3. She became a spy for the North.
4. She worked in the home of Jefferson Davis.
5. She passed along reports at secret meetings.

IMPROVING YOUR VOCABULARY

Choose the best word in Column B to complete each sentence in Column A. Use each word in Column B only once.

A

1. People came to the Awards Dinner to . . . . . . the best player on the team.
2. Alice became a . . . . when she saved the life of her crippled brother.
3. A great painter is not always . . . . for his fine work while he is alive.
4. The . . . . of the American Civil War should be known by every student.
5. Many . . . . were read during the meeting.

B

(a) heroine
(b) history
(c) reports
(d) honor
(e) recognized

SPELL IT RIGHT

Some words end in *e*. This final *e* is almost always silent. For example, the word *brave* in the story has a final, silent *e*. When you say the word, you do not sound the *e*.

A. Copy each of these words. Then underline the

silent *e* at the end of each word. The first one is done for you.

1. large   large_
2. home
3. life
4. true
5. made

B. Write the word in each pair which is spelled right. Don't look back.

1. life, lif
2. mayd, made
3. hom, home
4. large, larg
5. tru, true

C. Fill in the missing letter in each word.

1. tru . .
2. lar . . e
3. lif . .
4. ma . . e
5. hom . .

D. One of these five words is spelled wrong. Pick out the wrong word and spell it right.

life   large   made   tru   home

EXPRESSING YOURSELF

1. What is the difference between someone who is a spy for your country and someone who spies against your country?
2. Why do you think Mary Elizabeth Bowser was able to spy against the South and get away with it? Since she could not read or write, how could she work as a spy? Can a person be smart even if he or she does not know how to read or write? Explain.

3. Does it make sense to recognize Mary Elizabeth Bowser for something that took place over 100 years ago? Why?
4. A spy who is caught during a war is usually shot. Being a spy is a very dangerous thing to do. Tell why you think Mary Elizabeth did it.
5. Mary Ann Cary, Sarah Mapps Douglass, and Charlotta G. Pyles were active in the Civil War. Ask in your library for information about one of them. Tell what you learned.

WRITE NOW!

Write a paragraph about something or somebody you would put your life in danger for.

Begin by writing your own topic sentence. Then, finish with a sentence such as: "There are few things I'd put my life in danger for, but that is one." You can use that sentence, or make up a sentence of your own.

12. TEEN MODEL SAYS IT'S HARD WORK

DIGGING A DITCH IS A HARD JOB. LOADING A TRUCK IS A HARD JOB. IS HAVING YOUR PICTURE TAKEN A HARD JOB?

ISA LORENZO SAYS YES. WHAT COULD SHE MEAN?

The pretty young *model* stood on a New York City street corner. She would wave at a *taxi* as if she wanted one to stop. But the model didn't really want a taxi. She was just having her picture taken by a *photographer*. Taxis would stop, but the girl wouldn't get in.

"Did you ever see an angry taxi driver?" asked the model, Isa Lorenzo.

It's all in a day's work for Isa, who is 18 years old. As she put it, "Being a model is harder work than people would ever think."

Isa says that models must be moving all day long. The photographer is always telling them to look this way, to move that way. "You're just going and going and going," she said. She *often* works from 7:30 in the morning until 7:30 at night, and then takes the railroad home.

Isa thinks it is hard to work under the hot lights all day. After a while, her eyes begin to hurt. The lights used for TV ads are the hottest ones. When you work under them, it's like being out on the hottest day.

She must get along with many different kinds of people and always be *calm* with them. She must do so even if she doesn't feel like it at the time. "If you want to work, people have to like you," she says.

"The models aren't perfect, but they're made to look like it. It's a *dreamland*," she said of the modeling world. To get one picture that will be used, the photographers will often take 500 pictures.

Why does she work as a model when the work is so hard? "Everybody wants to be *rich* and *famous*. The modeling world can make that dream come true."

She *plans* to give up modeling in a year or two. She goes to school at night now and hopes some day to be a *doctor*.

—BELLMORE (N.Y.) LIFE

CHECK YOUR UNDERSTANDING

1. Isa often works from 7:30 in the morning until
    (A) 7:30 at night
    (B) 5:30 at night
    (C) 7:30 the next morning
2. Isa works hard as a model because she wants to
    (A) be perfect
    (B) be rich and famous
    (C) enjoy life
3. The lights used for TV ads are very
    (A) cool
    (B) hot
    (C) thick
4. Isa plans to
    (A) marry a taxi driver
    (B) give up modeling in a year or two
    (C) become a photographer
5. Which title tells most about the story?
    (A) Getting Taxi Drivers Angry
    (B) Working Hard to Be Rich and Famous
    (C) Studying to be a Doctor

FIND THE MISSING WORD

In your notebook, complete the following sentences with words from the story. You may look back at the story.

1. Isa would wave at a . . . .
2. Models are made to look perfect, like they are in a . . . .
3. Isa hopes to become a . . . .
4. She . . . . to give up modeling in a year or two.

5. Everybody wants to be . . . . . . and famous.

WHAT'S THE REASON?

When you read, you sometimes have to be a good detective. You have to find out *why* things happen. See if you can find the right "why" to answer each of these questions.

1. The taxi drivers became angry because Isa
   (A) did not see them
   (B) wanted to take their picture
   (C) wouldn't get in when they stopped
2. Modeling is hard work because models must
   (A) be moving all day long
   (B) get their picture taken
   (C) wear make-up
3. Isa thinks that she must get along with different kinds of people in order to
   (A) have her pictures look beautiful
   (B) get work as a model
   (C) prove she is honest
4. Photographers will often take 500 pictures to get one picture that will be used because they
   (A) get paid for each picture they take
   (B) want the model to work hard
   (C) want the model to look perfect

IMPROVING YOUR VOCABULARY

At the top of the next page choose the best word in Column B to complete each sentence in Column A. Use each word in Column B only once.

A	**B**
1. One night the . . . . was broken by a loud BOOM.	(a) photographer
	(b) famous
	(c) calm
2. If you . . . . ar-rive late to work, you might lose your job.	(d) model
	(e) often
3. The . . . . took pictures for the school newspaper.	
4. The person who dis-covers a cure for cancer will become	
5. The handsome . . . . . . wore fine clothing for the necktie ad.	

SPELL IT RIGHT

In the last lesson, we learned that an *e* at the end of a word is almost always silent. Which of these two words from the story has a silent *e*: *wave* or *get*?

One way to learn to spell better is to break longer words into sounds, or syllables (SILL uh bulls). When you break a word up, you can then learn one sound at a time. Often, a sound is one you can already spell.

Most of the time, there is one syllable for every vowel (*a,e,i,o,u,* and sometimes *y*) that is sounded. For example, the word *taken* in the story has two sounded vowels: *a* and *e*. *Taken,* then, has two syl-lables: *ta/ken.*

A. Copy each of these words. Then underline each vowel. Next to each word write the number of syllables it has. The first one is done for you.
1. corner   corner 2 (2 vowels—2 syllables)
2. driver
3. angry (count the *y* as a vowel)
4. always (here the *y* is not a vowel)
5. perfect

B. Write the word in each pair which is spelled right. Don't look back.
1. angery, angry
2. driver, drivar
3. purfect, perfect
4. allways, always
5. corner, cornir

C. Fill in the missing letter in each word.
1. co . . ner
2. angr . .
3. perfe . . t
4. driv . . r
5. alwa . . s

D. One of these five words is spelled wrong. Pick out the wrong word and spell it right.

    driver   perfict   corner   angry   always

EXPRESSING YOURSELF

1. Why do photographers have pretty women and handsome men as models? Why do companies want to show such people in their ads?
2. If the job is so hard, why does Isa Lorenzo remain a model? If someone asked you to be a model, what would you say? Why?

3. "If you want to work, people have to like you," Isa said. What does she mean? Do you care how others feel about you? Is it more important to be good at your job, or to be well-liked? Explain.
4. Pick someone in your class who could be a model. Take that person's picture and then make up an ad to go with the picture. You might be selling clothes, cars, food, etc.

WRITE NOW!

Write a paragraph on one of these topics:

> The Prettiest Woman
> The Handsomest Man
> It Was Hard Work
> A Picture I'd Like to Take

13. "MR. KOOL"

POLICEMAN GREGORY FOSTER WAS "MR. KOOL" TO 11 KIDS.

WHY WILL HE BE REMEMBERED?

Eleven boys used to play baseball and basketball in the playground with police officer Gregory Foster. They called him "Mr. Kool." But, Foster and another policeman were *shot* down. Both *died*. The eleven boys *wrote* a letter to "Mr. Kool," remembering their friend. It was left at the *funeral*.

The letter reads:

"Mr. Kool, if it ever looks like I'm getting my-self into trouble, I'll close my eyes and I'll believe that I see you walking down the *avenue*. As always, you'll be going into our *clubhouse* and asking us, 'Are you keeping kool, kids?'

"I'll always remember when you played bas-ketball and baseball in the summer with us in 12th Street Park. I still have my glove and I remember the last time you used it to *pitch* part of a game. Every time you heard about some kids in trouble you used to look for us and make sure that we had no part of it.

"I will always remember your last words to us: keep out of trouble. 'Hey guys, stay kool.' We know that you are still with us walking down the avenue and keeping us kool. We'll miss you and we'll never *forget* you, because we are sure you'll be beside us. From now on all the other cops will be 'Mr. Kool' to us, but *none* as kool as you."

The letter was signed by Jose Siguero, David Corrian, Rubin Colon, Paul Rosaro, George Rivera, Jose Leon, Eddie Torres, Johnny Perez, Eddie Bera, Carlos Rivera, and Miguel Belanco.

—NEW YORK TIMES

CHECK YOUR UNDERSTANDING

1. "Stay kool" means
   - (A) play ball
   - (B) stay out of trouble
   - (C) buy a cool drink
2. The person who said, "Hey guys, stay kool," is
   - (A) "Mr. Kool"
   - (B) Rubin Colon
   - (C) Carlos Rivera

3. Eleven boys wrote a letter to Gregory Foster because

(A) he was dying

(B) they wanted to remember him and his good advice

(C) they were in trouble

4. The boys say that they will stay out of trouble by

(A) playing ball with Gregory Foster

(B) thinking that Gregory Foster is still with them, keeping them cool

(C) writing a letter

5. Which title tells most about the story?

(A) Remembering a Good Friend

(B) Meeting in a Clubhouse

(C) Baseball and Other Games

FIND THE MISSING WORD

In your notebook, complete the following sentences with words from the story. You may look at the story.

1. Gregory Foster and another policeman were . . . . down.

2. Policeman Gregory Foster walked down the . . . .

3. He would play baseball and basketball with . . . . boys.

4. Gregory Foster often visited the eleven boys in their . . . .

5. When he . . . ., the boys wrote a letter to remember their friend.

FIRST THINGS FIRST

The 11 boys wrote a letter to policeman Gregory Foster. Arrange these events in the order they were said in the letter.

1. I'll always remember how you played basketball and baseball with us in 12th Street Park.
2. I'll close my eyes and believe I see you walking down the avenue.
3. From now on all the other cops will be 'Mr. Kool' to us, but none as cool as you.
4. I remember the last time you used my glove to pitch part of a game.
5. I will always remember your last words to us: keep out of trouble.

IMPROVING YOUR VOCABULARY

Choose the best word in Column B to complete each sentence in Column A. Use each word in Column B only once.

A	B
1. Flowers were sent to the .... home.	(a) none
	(b) pitch
2. .... of the eleven boys will ever forget Mr. Kool.	(c) forget
	(d) wrote
3. The coach of our team used to .... part of a game.	(e) funeral
4. We'll miss you and we'll never .... you.	
5. The boys .... a letter to a real friend, policeman Gregory Foster.	

SPELL IT RIGHT

In the last lesson, we learned that in learning to spell longer words we should break the words into syllables. We also learned that most of the time, there are as many syllables as there are sounded vowels. How many syllables are there in the word *ever*?

When two consonants come together and both consonants are the same letter, the word is broken up between the two consonants. For example, the word *winner* has two *n*'s next to each other. The word is broken up as *win/ner*.

A. Copy each of these words. Then, put a slanted line after the letter that ends the first syllable. The first word is done for you.

1. letter   let/ter
2. getting
3. summer
4. pretty
5. hottest

B. Write the word in each pair which is spelled right. Don't look back.

1. summer, sumer
2. prety, pretty
3. hotest, hottest
4. letter, leter
5. geting, getting

C. Fill in the missing letter in each word.

1. hot . . est
2. lett . . r
3. su . . mer
4. prett . .
5. get . . ing

D. One of these five words is spelled wrong. Pick out the wrong word and spell it right.

hotest   getting   summer   letter   pretty

EXPRESSING YOURSELF

1. Why did the boys take the trouble to write to the dead policeman? Since the boys seem to be good spellers, why didn't they spell it "Mr. Cool"?
2. What did Gregory Foster mean when he told the boys to be cool? Is it a good thing to be that way? Tell of a time when you should have been cool.
3. Should a policeman be playing ball with kids or should he be out catching crooks? Why do you think Gregory Foster spent so much time with young fellows?

WRITE NOW!

1. What would Gregory Foster say to the boys if he could answer their letter? Write a letter for Gregory Foster to the boys.
2. Write a paragraph on one of these topics:

    A Police Officer I Like
    Keeping Cool
    A Friend I Will Always Remember

14. FROM COP TO DOC

AT AGE 21 JOHN ANDINO WAS STILL IN HIGH SCHOOL.

WOULD HIS DREAM OF BEING A DOCTOR EVER COME TRUE?

The turning point in John Andino's life took place over 30 years ago. He was 21, just back from four years in World War II. He returned to high school in Brooklyn, four years older than most of the other *students*.

His teacher asked him to cover his books. He *refused*. Then, once, he came in late. The teacher asked for a note from his mother.

"My mother!" Andino shouted at the teacher. "My mother! You're kidding. I'm 21 years old. I'm old enough to *vote*. I've been in a *war*."

Then, he says, the best thing that ever happened to him took place. The teacher reported him to Abe Lass. Lass dropped the idea of telling John's mother. He came across other students like John, who had been in the war. He set up a special catch-up class just for them.

"I could have gone *either* way," remembers Andino. "One of my friends is still in *jail*. Another was killed. That sort of thing. But Abe got me going."

Abe Lass remembers that class very well. He remembers how on edge the students were. Many of them had almost been killed. He remembers telling them, "I didn't start the war. I didn't make you *lose* years of your life. But I will try and give you back part of your life if you try, too."

John Andino tried hard. Mr. Lass helped get him into *college*. John stayed there for two years, hoping to be a doctor. But it took too much money to stay in school and too long to become a doctor. He *became* a teacher. Then he became a cop.

He was a policeman for 14 years. But, he still wanted to be a doctor. Ten years ago he left the police force. For ten years, with the help of his wife, he *studied* so that he might be a doctor. This year he started a new life. He was 51 years old and had finally made it. His dream had come true. He was a doctor. And it all started 30 years ago when his teacher reported him to Abe Lass.

—NEW YORK TIMES

CHECK YOUR UNDERSTANDING

1. The person who helped John when he went to high school was
   (A) Abe Lass
   (B) John's mother
   (C) John's teacher
2. John became a doctor when he was
   (A) 21 years old
   (B) 31 years old
   (C) 51 years old
3. Abe Lass helped John Andino in high school by
   (A) speaking to his mother
   (B) setting up a special catch-up class
   (C) giving him money to go to college
4. The turning point in John Andino's life happened when
   (A) his friend got killed
   (B) he was reported to Abe Lass
   (C) he became a doctor
5. Which title tells most about the story?
   (A) The Problems of a Policeman
   (B) John Andino's Dream Comes True
   (C) How to Get Through School

FIND THE MISSING WORD

In your notebook, complete the following sentences with words from the story. You may look at the story.

1. John Andino .... a teacher, a cop, and a doctor.
2. "I could have gone .... way," he said.

3. One of my friends is still in . . . .

4. Mr. Lass told his class, "I didn't make you . . . . years of your life."

5. John Andino was in World . . . . II.

FIRST THINGS FIRST

Arrange these events in the order in which they really happened to John Andino.

1. John Andino came back from World War II.

2. John Andino became a doctor.

3. A teacher reported John for lateness.

4. Mr. Lass helped John to get into college.

5. A special class was set up for older students.

IMPROVING YOUR VOCABULARY

Choose the best word in Column B to complete each sentence in Column A. Use each word in Column B only once.

A	B
1. John Andino . . . . to cover his books.	(a) students
	(b) studied
2. Many . . . . had special problems when they returned to classes.	(c) college
	(d) vote
	(e) refused
3. To go to . . . . , you must receive a diploma from high school.	
4. A doctor has . . . . for many years in school.	
5. When you become 18, you have the right to	

94

SPELL IT RIGHT
Review of Words from Lessons 10-13

A. There is one word spelled wrong in each line. Pick out that word and spell it right.

1. allways, working, walking, angry
2. true, corner, driver, sumer
3. going, getting, pretty, perfict
4. pulling, made, helpin, home
5. large, life, hotest, letter

B. Choose the best answer for each of the following questions.

1. Which one of these words has two syllables?
   (A) Most (B) High (C) Ago (D) Than
2. Which one of these is a compound word?
   (A) Become (B) Asked (C) Note (D) Turning
3. Which of these words has two vowels together, with one vowel silent?
   (A) Dropped (B) Dream (C) Might (D) Happened
4. Which of these words is in the past time?
   (A) Enough (B) Point (C) Killed (D) Idea
5. Which of these words has a homonym?
   (A) Shouted (B) Too (C) Edge (D) Money
6. Which of these words is broken up into syllables after the letter *p*?
   (A) Point (B) Place (C) Special (D) Happen
7. Which of these words has a silent letter at the end?
   (A) Note (B) Point (C) Doctor (D) Dream

8. Which of these words is a contraction?
   (A) Once (B) Didn't (C) Than (D) Older

EXPRESSING YOURSELF

1. One man, Abe Lass, did a great deal for John
   Andino. Tell about the one person who has done
   the most for you so far in life.
2. Why did Abe Lass want to help boys such as
   John? Why didn't all of John's friends make it
   the way he did?
3. Do you think John Andino could be as good a
   doctor as someone who is much younger? Why?
   Would you want him to be your doctor? Why?
4. Suppose a doctor wanted to be a teacher or a
   policeman. Should he or she do it or should that
   person stay a doctor? Why?

WRITE NOW!

Write a paragraph on one of these topics:

> A Teacher Who Helped Me
> A Turning Point
> A Dream Come True

96

15. ALL-AROUND ACTRESS

DWAN SMITH CAN DO IT ALL:
ACT, DANCE, SING, WRITE.

HOW DO THE WORDS OF HER SONG
HOLD THE KEY TO HER LIFE?

"Ain't gonna never get old,
  I got love in my heart,
  And joy in my soul,
  I got faith in tomorrow,
  And hope for today,
  That's what makes me feel that way . . ."

These words were written by Dwan Smith, songwriter. Then there is Dwan Smith, singer; Dwan Smith, dancer; Dwan Smith, book writer; Dwan Smith, actress. Add Dwan Smith, mother, and Dwan Smith, youth worker. You *wonder* where one woman can find the time to do all these things.

You've seen her on TV. She has been on more than 50 TV ads. She's also acted in "Sanford and Son," "The Mary Tyler Moore Show," "The Name of the Game," and other TV shows.

She has a night club *act* where she sings, tells a few jokes, and dances. She has written a book. She has written a play for the movies. But why go on? What is Dwan Smith's secret?

She says there really is no secret. "It's hard and it takes a lot of *luck* and even more hard work. I've had good luck and I've worked hard and the breaks are beginning to come my way. . . . I just decided I was going to be good and took nothing *less* from myself."

Dwan Smith is proud of her three-year-old *daughter,* Ayanna BiBi. The girl's name is East African, and means, "beautiful flower, daughter of a king." Ms. Smith plans what she does around her daughter. "I'm at home when she goes to bed and there when she wakes up. If I *travel* out of town, she goes with me. There is no one who can take the place of a mother."

Dwan Smith is also the head of a club for people between the ages of 12 and 18. The club helps young people get ahead. All the money for it is raised by Ms. Smith.

As an actress, she sees herself as a model for young people to look up to and maybe even try to take after. She says, "I couldn't set a bad *example* for them. I once did a *wine* ad that I was unhappy with. It didn't do anything to keep young people from drinking. I wouldn't do it again."

What does she do in her *free* time? "I don't have any free time," she says. "Sounds crazy, but I *enjoy* every minute of my busy life. I can't think of anything I would change in my life. And things look better for me each day."

It's all there in these words:

"Ain't gonna never get old,
 I got love in my heart,
 And joy in my soul,
 I got faith in tomorrow,
 And hope for today,
 That's what makes me feel that way. . . ."

—MILWAUKEE JOURNAL

CHECK YOUR UNDERSTANDING

1. Dwan Smith's song tells that she believes in having
   (A) one true love
   (B) no secrets
   (C) faith and hope
2. Dwan Smith is *not* a
   (A) grandmother
   (B) dancer
   (C) book writer
3. The name Ayanna BiBi means
   (A) beloved of the Lord
   (B) she who walks with grace
   (C) beautiful flower, daughter of a king
4. The purpose of the club for young people is to
   (A) raise money for Ms. Smith
   (B) help young people
   (C) provide schooling

5. Which title tells most about the story?
- (A) Acting on TV
- (B) Mother and Daughter
- (C) Enjoying a Busy Life

FIND THE MISSING WORD

In your notebook, complete the following sentences with words from the story. You may look back at the story.

1. Dwan has a night club . . . .
2. It takes a lot of . . . . and hard work to become famous.
3. What does she do in her . . . . time?
4. Dwan decided she was going to be good and took nothing . . . . from herself.
5. She was not happy about a . . . . ad.

WHAT'S THE REASON?

When you read, you sometimes have to be a good detective. You have to find out *why* things happen. See if you can find the right "why" to answer each of these questions.

1. Dwan Smith wants to spend as much time as she can with her daughter because she
- (A) feels it will help her night club act
- (B) is proud of her daughter
- (C) doesn't like her work

2. Dwan Smith raises money for her club for young people because she
- (A) wants to help young people get ahead
- (B) feels she can make money from the club
- (C) feels it will help her in her work

100

3. Dwan was unhappy with a wine ad because
  (A) not enough people saw it
  (B) she didn't get enough money for it
  (C) it didn't do anything to keep young people from drinking
4. Dwan enjoys life because she
  (A) does not work hard
  (B) likes what she is doing
  (C) is seen by many people

IMPROVING YOUR VOCABULARY

Choose the best word in Column B to complete each sentence in Column A. Use each word in Column B only once.

A	B
1. I .... when Dwan Smith will make a movie.	(a) enjoy
	(b) example
2. Dwan Smith has a three-year-old	(c) travel
	(d) wonder
3. The children .... eating their ice cream cones.	(e) daughter
4. Can we see an .... of your card tricks?	
5. Fred likes to .... by airplane.	

SPELL IT RIGHT

Most of the time, if you see an *s* at the end of a verb (an action word) it means that the verb is being used with a singular noun (a name word that stands for only one person, place, or thing).

For example, in the story we read that *Dwan Smith sings*. Dwan Smith is only one person, so we have an *s* at the end of *sings*. If we were talking about more than one person, place, or thing, there would not be an *s* at the end of the verb. For example, you would say that *Dwan and her daughter sing,* since Dwan and her daughter make up two people.

A. Write the word in the parentheses that would make the sentence right. The first one is done for you.

1. The music (sound/sounds) good. (The right answer is *sounds* since music is only one.)
2. Dwan (dance/dances) well.
3. She (plan/plans) to go into the movies.
4. Bob (wake/wakes) early in the morning.
5. She (say/says) there is no secret to her success.

B. Write the word in each pair which is spelled right. Don't look back.

1. plans, planns
2. says, sez
3. dancis, dances
4. sownds, sounds
5. wakes, waks

C. Fill in the missing letter in each word.

1. danc . s
2. plan . .
3. so . . nds
4. wak . . s
5. sa . . s

D. One of these five words is spelled wrong. Pick out the wrong word and spell it right.

sownds   dances   says   plans   wakes

EXPRESSING YOURSELF

1. Dwan Smith's song holds the key to her life. What hints does it give you about why Dwan is successful?
2. Write the words of a song that tell what is important in your life.
3. A woman like Dwan is building a career and raising a family. Both of these are full-time jobs. Do you think you can do both? Tell of some of the problems you will face. If you don't think you can do both, which might you prefer—a career or raising a family? Why?
4. Dwan sees herself as a model for young people to look up to. Imagine that you became successful like her. What would you do to help young people?

WRITE NOW!

Dwan Smith leads a full life and enjoys every minute of it. Write a paragraph telling what your idea of a full life is. Write your own topic sentence. Your final sentence could be: *A life like that would make me happy.* (If you don't like that as your last sentence, make up one of your own.)

REVIEW OF LESSONS 11-15

FINDING THE MISSING WORD

The sentences below are followed by a list of *italicized* words. For each sentence, write the word that fits best in the blank. Use each word only once. (The number in parentheses tells you the number of the story in which the word was first used.)

1. What famous woman would you . . . . for her fine work in sports?
2. A . . . . who is caught during a war will be killed.
3. A . . . . must stand still under hot lights for many hours.

4. Driving a . . . . for many hours is usually very tiring.
5. His best . . . . is a fastball.
6. Our football team has . . . . great players
and a super coach.
7. Bobby Fischer . . . . and played many
chess games to become one of the best players
in the world.
8. . . . . you win or you lose in the play-off
games.
9. To which countries will you plan to . . . .
when you go away?
10. In order to receive an Oscar award, you must
. . . . unusually well.

(a) *act* (15)   (f) *pitch* (13)
(b) *travel* (15)   (g) *taxi* (12)
(c) *studied* (14)   (h) *model* (12)
(d) *either* (14)   (i) *spy* (11)
(e) *eleven* (13)   (j) *honor* (11)

FINDING THE OPPOSITE

For each of the words in capitals, choose the
word on the right that is most nearly OPPOSITE.
(The number in parentheses tells you the number of
the story in which the word was first used.)

1. WONDER (15)   (A) lose (B) know
                  (C) prepare
2. CALM (12)   (A) upset (B) cool
                  (C) quiet
3. DIED (13)   (A) worked (B) played
                  (C) lived
4. LESS (15)   (A) more (B) few (C)
                  half

5. LOSE (14) (A) tight (B) win (C) fix

6. NONE (13) (A) some (B) not a one (C) all

7. RECEIVE (11) (A) give (B) take (C) gone

8. RECOGNIZE (11) (A) know (B) leave (C) forget

9. REFUSED (14) (A) said yes (B) said no (C) said maybe

10. RICH (12) (A) sweet (B) right (C) poor

UNSCRAMBLING THE WORD

Each of the definitions below is followed by a scrambled word that fits the meaning. Unscramble the letters to find the word. (The number in parentheses tells you the number of the story in which the word was first used.)

1. the story of a person or a country (11) SITHORY

2. coming together (11) ETINGEM

3. a person who knows how to take care of the sick (12) TORCOD

4. very well known (12) AMOFUS

5. a wide street (13) EAVUNE

6. made letters or words (13) TROWE

7. came to be; grew to be (14) ACEBEM

8. a place for people who break the law (14) ILAJ

9. father's or mother's girl (15) THERGAUD

10. be happy with (15) JONEY

FINDING THE RIGHT MEANING

Match each word in Column A to the best meaning in Column B. (The number in parentheses tells you the number of the story in which the word was first used.)

A	B
1. CLUBHOUSE (13)	(A) place for club to meet (B) place for dances (C) place for eating
2. COLLEGE (14)	(A) a school for higher learning (B) a school that gives free instruction (C) a school that gives jobs to students
3. EXAMPLE (15)	(A) a thing which is broken (B) a thing which shows what other things are like (C) a thing that moves
4. FUNERAL (13)	(A) help given to a live person (B) acts in honor of a person who has died (C) things done for fun
5. HEROINE (11)	(A) a girl hero (B) a boy hero (C) an animal hero
6. LUCK (15)	(A) that which happens by accident (B) that which is nearby (C) that which never happens
7. OFTEN (12)	(A) few times (B) sometimes (C) many times

8. PHOTOG-
RAPHER (12)
(A) a person who paints pictures (B) a person who buys pictures (C) a person who takes pictures with a camera

9. PRESIDENT (11)
(A) the highest job in a company (B) a person who writes letters (C) a person who takes money

10. STUDENT (14)
(A) person who teaches in a school (B) person who learns in a school (C) person who leaves a school

16. DOG RESCUES MASTER FROM CREEK

IS A DOG A PERSON'S BEST FRIEND?

GARY SALTZ HAS A DOG
AND YOU MAY WANT ONE TOO,
AFTER YOU READ THIS STORY.

Gary Saltz and his dog Hal were enjoying a spring afternoon. They were by the Ohio River, where Cane Run *Creek* empties into it.

Hal is a three-year-old, 240-pound St. Bernard. He was off by himself. The mouth of the creek was *packed* with driftwood.* It looked safe,

---

* Driftwood — wood floating in or washed ashore by water.

so Saltz thought he'd try to walk across.

He stepped carefully from *log* to log. Suddenly, two big logs moved *apart.* Saltz found himself in the creek.

The water was up to his *chest,* and he couldn't *touch* bottom. He kept *grabbing* for a log to hold onto, but the logs kept rolling away. He couldn't get out of the water. He was about 20 feet from *shore.*

"I called for my dog," Saltz said. "I whistled and he started barking."

Hal, the hero, went to work. He made his way over the driftwood to Saltz. Saltz reached for him, and Hal grabbed the arm of Saltz's coat with his *teeth.*

"He *dragged* me out. He really and truly dragged me 16 feet to where there were finally enough logs packed together that I could grab hold of something," Saltz said. "All those stories that have ever been told about St. Bernards are true. Those dogs know when you're in trouble, and they come and get you. I'd never believed about dogs doing things for people out of love, but it happened. He did it, he really did it. This has been an afternoon I'll never forget."

—LOUISVILLE COURIER-JOURNAL

CHECK YOUR UNDERSTANDING

1. Gary Saltz got into trouble when he tried to
   (A) make his dog go across the river
   (B) walk across a creek packed with logs
   (C) swim across the Ohio River

2. After Saltz fell in the water he
   (A) could not touch the bottom
   (B) held onto a log
   (C) lost sight of land
3. Saltz couldn't get out of the water because
   (A) logs were in the way
   (B) he didn't know how to swim
   (C) he was a mile from shore
4. The St. Bernard saved Saltz by
   (A) barking until a man named Hal came by
   (B) dragging him to where there were enough logs to hold onto
   (C) bringing Saltz a boat
5. Which title tells most about the story?
   (A) It's True What They Say About St. Bernards
   (B) Log Rolling on Cane Run Creek
   (C) Enjoying a Spring Afternoon

FIND THE MISSING WORD

In your notebook, complete the following sentences with words from the story. You may look back at the story.

1. Cane Run . . . . empties into the Ohio River.
2. The mouth of the creek was . . . . with driftwood.
3. Saltz kept grabbing for a . . . . to hold onto.
4. The water was up to his . . . .
5. Hal grabbed the arm of Saltz's coat with his . . . .

FIRST THINGS FIRST

Arrange these events in the order in which they really happened.

1. Saltz whistled for Hal, who started barking.
2. Hal grabbed Saltz's coat with his teeth.
3. Hal dragged Saltz out to where he could grab hold of some logs.
4. Saltz found himself in water up to his chest.
5. Saltz tried to walk across the mouth of Cane Run Creek.

IMPROVING YOUR VOCABULARY

Choose the best word in Column B to complete each sentence in Column A. Use each word in Column B only once.

A	B
1. We .... the heavy table across the floor.	(a) shore
2. Each person stood one foot .... from the next person.	(b) apart (c) dragged
3. Ruth and Danny walked across the .... into the water.	(d) touch (e) grabbing
4. Len kept .... for the balloon and it kept flying away from him.	
5. Don't .... anything because the room has just been painted.	

SPELL IT RIGHT

In the last lesson, we learned that an *s* at the end of a verb means that the noun it goes with is singular (only one). Would you say *The dog know* or *The dog knows*?

Almost always, *ly* at the end of a word tells you that that word will say *how* something happened. For example, in the sentence *Ira ran quickly*, *quickly* tells you *how* Ira ran. The *ly* is added to the adjective (describing word) *quick*.

A. Write the word to which *ly* has been added. The first one is done for you.
1. safely   *safe*
2. suddenly
3. really
4. truly (clue: an *e* has been dropped before the *ly*)
5. finally

B. Write the word in each pair which is spelled right. Don't look back.
1. sudenly, suddenly
2. finaly, finally
3. safely, safly
4. realy, really
5. truely, truly

C. Fill in the missing letter in each word.
1. re . lly
2. sud . enly
3. tru . y
4. saf . ly
5. fin . lly

D. One of these five words is spelled wrong. Pick out the wrong word and spell it right.

really   truly   finaly   suddenly   safely

1. How did Hal know that Gary was really in trouble and not just playing with him? Are dogs smart animals? How can you tell?
2. Go to your library and read about St. Bernards. In what ways have they helped people?
3. You may have seen Lassie or other dogs on TV or in the movies. Tell about a time when such a dog saved people who were in trouble.
4. If you had been with Gary Saltz that day, what would you have done to save him? Tell of a time when you or someone you know helped save another person's life.
5. Would a human being put his own life in danger to save his dog just as the St. Bernard did to save Gary? Make up a story in which an animal is facing death and someone risks his own life to save the animal.

WRITE NOW!

Write a paragraph on one of these topics:

> My Favorite Pet
> I Don't Like Animals
> Saving a Life

Make up your own topic sentence for the paragraph you write.

17. BLACKENED LAND GETS NEW LIFE

WE USE FIRE TO COOK OUR FOOD AND KEEP US WARM BUT FIRE CAN BE MISUSED.

WHAT LESSON DID THE YMCA CAMPERS LEARN?

The *earth* at the YMCA * camp is coming to life. Everywhere you can see green leaves and bright May flowers. *However,* all around the bright, growing things are burned-out trees and bushes.

Last year, a fire at the camp burned for 12 weeks. It *destroyed* 15 to 20 *acres* of field and *forest*. This week, the same people who *caused* the fire came back to plant *thousands* of trees and

---

* YMCA — an abbreviation for Young Men's Christian Association. The YMCA runs many camps all over the United States.

bushes in the blackened earth. More than 200 of their school friends helped, too.

The fire began late last fall. A number of 12-year-olds were spending a day at the camp. Building fires was one thing they learned that day.

A few campers used a fire to try to *smoke* a gopher ** out of his hole. Nearby bushes caught fire. Before long, the hills were on fire. It took 12 weeks before the fire was finally all out.

The campers felt very bad about what had happened. Their school held *sales* to raise money. The school gave the YMCA about $275. That helped pay for 500 new trees.

Besides raising money, the campers said they would help plant the 11,500 seedlings *** the camp had bought. The seedlings would be planted to return life to the fields and woods. This week, as the campers planted, they could not help but remember the fire. Burned bushes, black grass and *dead* wood were all around them.

"Right now, the campers are learning something important," the head of the camp said. "They see all that has happened because of what they did without thinking."

—MILWAUKEE JOURNAL

** Gopher — a small animal that digs holes underground.
*** Seedling — a young plant.

CHECK YOUR UNDERSTANDING

1. The time of the year when the story was written is
(A) winter
(B) spring
(C) fall

2. The fire was caused by people
   (A) cooking soup over a campfire
   (B) throwing matches into a pile of leaves
   (C) trying to smoke a gopher from its hole
3. The people who caused the fire
   (A) were put in jail
   (B) never went back to the camp
   (C) helped plant new trees and bushes
4. The head of the YMCA camp
   (A) thought the campers had learned some-thing important
   (B) gave the school $250
   (C) would not let the people who started the fire help plant new trees
5. Which title tells most about the story?
   (A) A Little Fire That Destroyed Acres
   (B) Life at a YMCA Camp
   (C) Raising Money Through School Sales

FIND THE MISSING WORD

In your notebook, complete the following sentences with words from the story. You may look back at the story.

1. The . . . . at the YMCA camp is com-ing to life.
2. . . . ., all around the bright, growing things are burned-out trees and bushes.
3. A fire destroyed 15 to 20 . . . .
4. The campers came back to plant . . . . of trees and bushes.
5. A few campers used fire to try to . . . . a gopher out of his hole.

Arrange these events in the order in which they really happened.

1. A fire burned for 12 weeks.
2. The campers learned to build fires at the YMCA camp.
3. A few campers tried to smoke a gopher out of his hole.
4. The campers planted thousands of trees.
5. The school held sales to raise money.

IMPROVING YOUR VOCABULARY

Choose the best word in Column B to complete each sentence in Column A. Use each word in Column B only once.

A	B
1. The fire . . . . three houses.	(a) caused
2. There were many different kinds of trees in the	(b) dead
	(c) forest
3. The store had . . . . all week.	(d) destroyed
4. Many . . . . animals were found after the forest fire.	(e) sales
5. What . . . . you to be late for school this morning?	

118

SPELL IT RIGHT

When you want to show more than one of a noun (a word that names a person, place or thing), most of the time you add an *s* (or *es*) to the noun. For example, in this story, *friend* has been made plural by adding an *s* to make it *friends*.

A. Write the plural form of each of these nouns. The first one is done for you.
 1. flower   *flowers*
 2. tree
 3. fire
 4. bush
 5. hill

B. Write the word in each pair which is spelled right. Don't look back.
 1. flowers, flowrs
 2. hills, hils
 3. fiers, fires
 4. bushes, bushs
 5. tres, trees

C. Fill in the missing letter in each word.
 1. bush . .s
 2. tre . .s
 3. hi . ls
 4. flo . .ers
 5. fir . .s

D. One of these five words is spelled wrong. Pick out the wrong word and spell it right.
       bushs   hills   flowers   trees   fires

119

EXPRESSING YOURSELF

1. Why do you think the fire burned for 12 weeks? Why is it harder to put out a forest fire than a house fire in the city?

2. The head of the camp said that the fire took place "because of what they did without thinking." Tell of a time when you did something without thinking and it turned out bad.

3. What did the campers do to show that they were sorry about the fire? What lesson did they learn?

4. Make up your own poster, telling people to be careful about fire. It could have a saying such as, "Matches Don't Start Fires—People Do," or it could show a picture of some kind.

WRITE NOW!

Write a paragraph on one of these topics:

> Playing with Fire
> Sorry!
> Making Up for a Mistake

Remember to begin with your own topic sentence.

18. MEXICAN JUMPING BEANS

SEÑOR HERNANDEZ OF ALAMOS, MEXICO LOVES HIS MEXICAN JUMPING BEANS.

CAN YOU GUESS WHY?

ALAMOS, Mex. — How do jumping *beans* jump?

"Like this," said Joaquin Hernandez, 63, as he jumped over a pile of them. The beans were moving around on the floor of his house.

But why do they jump?

"Maybe for *exercise*. I don't really know," Hernandez *replied*.

The strange jumping seeds are known all over the world as Mexican jumping beans. In Mexico, they are called *los brincadores*. This means, "The jumpers."

It was Hernandez who first brought the beans to the world 51 years ago when he was a boy of 12. He has been the biggest seller of them from that time on.

Jumping beans are the seeds of a plant that grows wild in the foothills and mountains near Alamos. Alamos is a town with 3,500 people. The people of Alamos *harvest* the beans each June and July. The plants grow 10 to 20 feet high.

"Everybody in Alamos harvests the beans," *explained* Hernandez. "If a person is lucky he will make as much as 200 pesos ($16) in one day of picking."

The people of Alamos bring their jumping beans to Hernandez's house in the middle of the town. There, girls work for many weeks shaking and counting the beans. They shake each bean. If it *rattles,* it means the yellow *worm* inside is dead. The girls throw the "dead" beans away.

In a good year the people of Alamos and nearby towns harvest and sell more than 30 *million* jumping beans to Hernandez. His house sings with the sounds of millions of rattling, hopping beans. One huge room has jumping beans piled 2 feet deep. It is the biggest pile of jumping beans on earth.

"Only a few of the beans stay in Mexico," said Hernandez. "Most Mexicans have never heard of jumping beans. Just the people around here know them, and the people in the towns next to the United States, who see them for sale."

Hernandez tells how it all started. "An American came to Alamos in 1921. I sold him some *brincadores.* He was *amazed* by the jumping beans. He said he would buy as many beans as I could get him so he could sell them to other Americans.

"I got every kid in town to help me. That's how it started. The *brincadores* have put my 8 children through school."

Jumping beans are less than ⅓ of an inch long. A worm inside the *shell* keeps hitting its head against one end of the bean.

"We don't know why the worm inside moves around so much, but we are glad he does," said Hernandez.

"He isn't trying to get out. We know that for sure. If the shell is broken, the worm inside goes right to work to fix it. Then he starts jumping again, just like before."

A jumping bean can keep jumping for as long as 6 months. Then, when the worm is ready, it finally comes out of the shell.

—LOS ANGELES TIMES

CHECK YOUR UNDERSTANDING

1. Joaquin Hernandez is special because he
   - (A) was the first man to eat jumping beans
   - (B) is a boy of 12 who collects jumping beans
   - (C) is the biggest seller of Mexican jumping beans in the world

2. *Los Brincadores* is Spanish, meaning
   - (A) "the jumpers"
   - (B) "the worms"
   - (C) "the people"

3. Where do jumping beans grow?
   - (A) Near Alamos, Mexico
   - (B) All over the world
   - (C) All over Mexico

4. The worm inside a jumping bean stops jumping
   - (A) in hot weather
   - (B) when it is ready
   - (C) if the shell is broken

5. Which title tells most about the story?
   - (A) He Thanks the *Brincadores*
   - (B) A Small Mexican Town
   - (C) Earthworms

FIND THE MISSING WORD

In your notebook, complete the following sentences with words from the story. You may look back at the story.

1. How do jumping . . . . jump?
2. Maybe the beans jump for . . . .

124

3. The people of Alamos .... the beans each June and July.
4. If the bean rattles, the yellow .... inside is dead.
5. A worm inside the .... keeps hitting its head against one end of the bean.

WHAT'S THE REASON?

When you read, you sometimes have to be a good detective. You have to find out *why* things happen. See if you can find the right "why" to answer each of these questions.

1. Jumping beans jump because
    (A) there is a dead worm inside
    (B) a worm inside keeps hitting its head against one end of the bean
    (C) people want to make money from them
2. The girls throw away beans that rattle because
    (A) those beans are not good to eat
    (B) there is a live worm inside
    (C) those beans will not jump
3. The American bought many beans from Hernandez because he
    (A) liked to watch the beans jump
    (B) liked Hernandez
    (C) wanted to sell them to other Americans
4. Hernandez is glad the worm inside moves around so much because
    (A) if it didn't, Hernandez would not make money
    (B) it's better for the worm
    (C) it helps the beans grow bigger

BY THE NUMBERS

Numbers are used many times in this story. Choose the number from Column B which fits the description in Column A. Use each number in Column B only once.

A	**B**
1. Hernandez's age at the time this story was written	(a) ⅓ of an inch
2. The number of people in Alamos	(b) 6
3. The number of inches a jumping bean is long	(c) 8
4. How many feet high the jumping bean plants grow	(d) 10-20
5. How many pesos a lucky person can make in one day of picking the beans	(e) 63
6. The number of beans Hernandez will buy in a good year	(f) 200
7. The number of children Hernandez has	(g) 3,500
8. The number of months a jumping bean can keep jumping	(h) 30,000,000

IMPROVING YOUR VOCABULARY

At the top of the next page, choose the best word in Column B to complete each sentence in Column A. Use each word in Column B only once.

	A		**B**

A

1. What would you do with a . . . . dollars?
2. Babies love to play with . . . .
3. I was . . . . to see how high Paul could jump.
4. Don . . . . quickly to the teacher's question.
5. Sue . . . . how jumping beans jump.

B

(a) rattles
(b) replied
(c) explained
(d) amazed
(e) million

SPELL IT RIGHT

In the last lesson, we learned how to form the plural of most nouns. Does the word *beans* in this story mean one, or more than one?

In Lesson 3, we learned that two vowels sometimes come together in a word, and that one of the vowels can be silent. Sometimes, two vowels can come together to make a sound very much different from either of their usual sounds. For example, the word *sound* itself has two vowels together: *ou*. These two vowels often have the sound of *ow*, as in *now*.

A. Copy each of these words and underline the *ou* in each. The first one is done for you.

1. mountains mo<u>u</u>ntains
2. our
3. house
4. counting
5. around

B. Write the word in each pair which is spelled right. Don't look back.
1. mountains, mountans
2. counting, cownting
3. house, hous
4. ouer, our
5. around, aroun

C. Fill in the missing letter in each word.
1. o . . r
2. hous . .
3. co . . nting
4. ar . . und
5. mount . ins

D. One of these five words is spelled wrong. Pick out the wrong word and spell it right.

counting   house   our   around   mountins

EXPRESSING YOURSELF

1. Did you ever see a Mexican jumping bean? Why do people buy them?
2. If the beans grow in Mexico, why is it that most Mexicans have never heard of them? An American bought some beans from Senor Hernandez in 1921. What do you think the American did with the beans when he got them back to the United States?
3. Make believe you are selling those beans on TV. What would you say to people to make them want to buy your jumping beans?
4. Someone who lives in Alamos can make $16 for a hard day's work picking beans. Senor Hernandez does not pick beans but he makes at least ten times that much money every day. Why is that?

128

WRITE NOW!

Make believe that you are one of the jumping worms inside a Mexican jumping bean. Write a paragraph telling what you are thinking about as you jump up and down inside your shell. Now, imagine that you are the shell. Write a paragraph telling what you think as the worm jumps up and down inside you. Write what the worm and the shell say to each other.

19. LIGHTNING MAN

ROY SULLIVAN HAS BEEN STRUCK BY LIGHTNING SEVEN TIMES AND HE WANTS TO KNOW WHY.

HOW CAN HE KEEP HIMSELF SAFE?

Roy Sullivan is as *gentle* and good as a man can be. He pays his bills and loves his family. Roy is *honest* and has never *harmed* anyone. Why is it, then, that he has been struck by *lightning* seven times?

"I wish I knew," he said. "It's terrible. I don't believe God is after me. If He was, the first time would have been enough. I think that maybe my body *draws* lightning. I wish I knew."

Lightning has harmed him in many ways. It has knocked him out, burned off his hair and *damaged* his hearing. One time it tore off his shoe and a *toenail* under the shoe. Another time, it threw him into the air.

It has left him with a lot of damaged things such as a *melted* pocket watch and *shirts,* hats, and underwear with burn holes.

Sullivan had been a forest *ranger* at Shenandoah National Park in Virginia. He stopped working last year. Now he has placed 12 lightning rods * around the house he lives in. He hopes they will draw off any lightning that might be after him.

Good luck, Roy, but could you please stand over there while we talk?

—NEWSDAY (LONG ISLAND, N.Y.)

* Lightning rod — a metal rod placed high on a building. It draws lightning to the ground and keeps it from damaging the building.

CHECK YOUR UNDERSTANDING

1. What is unusual about Roy Sullivan?
   (A) Few people are as gentle and good as he is.
   (B) He has been struck by lightning many times.
   (C) He is the first person to live after being struck by lightning.
2. Roy Sullivan thinks that he has been struck by lightning so often because
   (A) God is after him
   (B) he's done something wrong
   (C) his body draws lightning

3. Roy Sullivan has placed 12 lightning rods around his house because he

    (A) hopes they will draw off lightning

    (B) was a forest ranger

    (C) thinks 12 is his lucky number

4. The last sentence of the story is meant to be funny. It means that the writer of the story does not

    (A) like Roy Sullivan

    (B) want to be hit by lightning

    (C) want to talk to Roy Sullivan

5. Which title tells most about the story?

    (A) A Forest Ranger

    (B) A Man Who Draws Lightning

    (C) A Good Man

FINDING THE MISSING WORD

In your notebook, complete the following sentences with words from the story. You may look back at the story.

1. Roy is . . . . and has never harmed anyone.

2. He thinks that maybe his body . . . . lightning.

3. Lightning tore off his shoe and a . . . . under the shoe.

4. Lightning has left him with . . . . , hats, and underwear with burn holes.

5. Sullivan had been a forest . . . . at Shenandoah National Park.

132

IMPROVING YOUR VOCABULARY

Choose the best word in Column B to complete each sentence in Column A. Use each word in Column B only once.

A	**B**
1. The . . . . came very close to hitting our house.	(a) melted
2. Brandy is such a . . . . dog it wouldn't hurt anyone.	(b) gentle
	(c) lightning
3. Our car was . . . . when the truck ran into it.	(d) harmed
3. When the sun came out, the snow	(e) damaged
5. Our team's chances of winning were . . . . when Tom broke his leg.	

SPELL IT RIGHT

Review of Words from Lessons 15-18

There is one word spelled wrong in each line. Pick out that word and spell it right.

1. says, realy, wakes, around
2. danses, bushes, trees, house
3. truly, counting, owr, mountains
4. safely, finally, plans, suddenley
5. sounds, flowrs, hills, fires

   In Lesson 5, we learned that *ed* at the end of the word means that the action is taking place in the past time. In this story, for example, *knocked* is past time for the present time verb *knock*. Also, *placed* is the past for the present-time verb *place*.

Not all verbs form their past time (past tense) simply by adding *ed* to the present time (present tense) form of the verb. Some verbs show past time in an *irregular* way. They do not add *ed*. They form past tense in a way for which there is no rule. You just have to learn to remember each past tense of each irregular verb. For example, take the present tense verb *know*. The past tense is NOT *knowed*. It is *knew*.

A. Match the present tense verb in Column A with its past tense in Column B. Write your answers in your notebook.

A	**B**
1. strike	(a) said
2. tear	(b) left
3. leave	(c) struck
4. say	(d) threw
5. throw	(e) tore

B. Write the word in each pair which is spelled right. Don't look back.
  1. said, sayed
  2. left, leaved
  3. tor, tore
  4. threw, thrue
  5. struck, struk

C. Fill in the missing letter in each word.
  1. le . t
  2. st . uck
  3. tor . .
  4. sa . d
  5. thr . w

134

D. One of these five words is spelled wrong. Pick out the wrong word and spell it right.

threw   said   left   struk   tore

EXPRESSING YOURSELF

1. What should you do if you are outside in a storm and there is lightning around? Why shouldn't you hide under a big tree?
2. Why does the story tell us that Roy is a good man who loves his family and is honest? Hint: Think about what this has to do with his being hit by lightning.
3. Why do you think that Roy has been hit by lightning so many times?
4. Roy has been a forest ranger. Go to the library and look up the work done by a forest ranger. Report back to the class. Would you like a job as a forest ranger?
5. Tell of a time when you or someone you know was, or was almost, harmed by lightning.

WRITE NOW!

Write a paragraph on one of these topics:

It Was Just My Luck
Out in a Storm
The Time I Got Hurt
Why Me?

20. BEES IN THE BEDROOM WALL

ONE FAMILY FOUND THAT THOUSANDS OF BEES WERE LIVING IN THE WALLS OF THEIR HOME.

WHAT DID THEY DO ABOUT IT?

Nick Troianello was starting some work on a bedroom in his family home. He cut a small hole in the outside wall and found *visitors*: bees.

Two beekeepers came to the Troianello home to get the bees out. They found 60,000 to 70,000 bees in the walls. One of the beekeepers said he had found four or five *hives* there. That was the most he had ever seen in one place. He said the bees had been there for many years, maybe as many as *twenty*.

The beekeepers were dressed in white. Their faces were covered with *netting*. They cut out the hive in pieces. They found that it covered two eight-foot-high parts of the wall. Each part was about 16 inches wide.

To make the bees easy to work with, the beekeepers burned rope. This made the bees think there was a forest fire and they *gathered* all the honey they could into their bodies. Then, they were like people who had overeaten. They became slow-moving and not *interested* in *stinging* anyone.

Many of the bees had gathered around the queen bee. They were there to keep her from harm and to keep warm by *sharing* body *heat*.

The beekeepers did not work alone. The Troianello family and their friends gathered near the second floor bedroom to watch the two men work. It took three hours for them to finish. That was because they took a good part of the time explaining what they were doing, and why.

The hives were moved to the backyard of one of the beekeepers. He said that most of the time you find 40 to 50 pounds of *delicious* honey in one hive.

Robert Troianello, 7, shared the bedroom with two older brothers. He said he wasn't afraid when he found out he was also sharing the bedroom with bees. That is, he wasn't afraid until he found out how many there were. He said he'd probably sleep in the living room that night.

—STATEN ISLAND (N.Y.) ADVANCE

CHECK YOUR UNDERSTANDING

1. When Nick Troianello cut a hole in the outside wall of his home, he found
- (A) bees
- (B) some people coming to visit him
- (C) two beekeepers

2. The beekeepers said
- (A) they had never seen so many bees in one place
- (B) the bees had been in the house for less than one year
- (C) they would not be able to get all the bees out

3. To make the bees easy to work with, the beekeepers
- (A) ate honey
- (B) moved slowly
- (C) burned rope

4. When the bees thought there was a forest fire, they
- (A) started stinging
- (B) gathered all the honey they could into their bodies
- (C) started to fly around quickly

5. Which title tells most about the story?
- (A) Making Honey
- (B) Getting the Bees Out
- (C) A Beekeeper's Life

FIND THE MISSING WORD

In your notebook, complete the following sentences with words from the story. You may look back at the story.

1. The beekeepers found four or five . . . . in the bedroom walls.
2. The bees had been there for as many as . . . . years.
3. The beekeepers' faces were covered with . . . .
4. The bees became slow-moving and not interested in . . . . anyone.
5. The bees tried to keep warm by sharing body . . . .

WHAT'S THE REASON?

When you read, you sometimes have to be a good detective. You have to find out *why* things happen. See if you can find the right "why" to answer each of these questions.

1. The beekeepers covered their faces with netting because they
   (A) were cold
   (B) did not want to be stung by bees
   (C) wanted to keep smoke out of their lungs
2. The bees became slow-moving and easy to work with because they
   (A) had overeaten
   (B) had been burned
   (C) were old

3. The bees gathered around the queen bee in order to

(A) get away from the beekeepers
(B) get away from the smoke
(C) keep warm and keep the queen bee safe

4. The Troianello family and their friends gathered near the second floor bedroom because they

(A) were going to help the beekeepers work
(B) wanted to stay away from the beekeepers
(C) were interested in watching the beekeepers work

5. Robert Troianello would probably sleep in the living room that night because

(A) he was afraid there would still be bees in the bedroom
(B) his brothers didn't want him with them anymore
(C) he hoped there would be bees in the living room

BY THE NUMBERS

Numbers are used many times in this story. At the top of the next page, choose the number from Column B which fits the description in Column A. Use each number in Column B only once.

	A		B
1.	Robert Troianello's age	(a)	4-5
2.	The number of bees in the walls	(b)	7
3.	The number of hives in the walls	(c)	8 feet by 16 inches
4.	The pounds of honey you get from a hive	(d)	20
5.	The size of each part of the wall that the hive covered	(e)	40-50
6.	The most number of years the beehive might have been in the walls	(f)	60,000-70,000

IMPROVING YOUR VOCABULARY

Choose the best word in Column B to complete each sentence in Column A. Use each word in Column B only once.

	A		B
1.	On Sunday, we had . . . . . . from out of town.	(a)	interested
2.	All her friends . . . . in Tina's house for a surprise birthday party.	(b)	visitors
		(c)	sharing
		(d)	gathered
3.	Glenn and Lori were . . . . in Anna's stories about her trip to Mexico.	(e)	delicious
4.	I have never eaten such . . . . home-made ice cream.		
5.	Nancy and Willa are . . . . the award for best player.		

141

SPELL IT RIGHT

In the last lesson, we learned how some verbs form their past tense in an irregular way. In this story, the past tense verb *found* is used. What is the present tense of *found*?

In Lesson 1, we learned about compound words. There are five more to learn from this story.

A. Write the two little words in each of these compound words.
   1. bedroom
   2. outside
   3. became
   4. anyone
   5. because

B. Write the one word in each pair which is spelled right. Don't look back.
   1. becaus, because
   2. outside, outsid
   3. anyone, enyone
   4. bedroom, bedrume
   5. becam, became

C. Fill in the missing letter in each word.
   1. an . . one
   2. bedro . . m
   3. becam . .
   4. outs . . de
   5. beca . . se

D. One of these five words is spelled wrong. Pick out the wrong word and spell it right.

   became   becawse   outside   anyone   bedroom

142

EXPRESSING YOURSELF

1. Are you uneasy when bees are around? What should you do to keep from being stung by a bee?
2. This story gives you interesting information about bees. For example, we read how the bees gathered around the queen bee to keep her from harm. Visit your library. Report back to the class on interesting facts you can find out about the life of a bee.
3. The Troianello family and their friends were interested in watching the beekeepers work. Tell about another kind of work you would find interesting to watch. Why?
4. Robert Troianello shares a room with two older brothers. How do you think he gets along with them? Tell how you get along with an older or younger brother or sister.
5. Some people think that honey right from the hive is delicious. What food do you find "delicious"?

WRITE NOW!

Many people are afraid of bees. Write a paragraph telling about something you are afraid of, or about some fear you used to have but have since gotten over.

REVIEW OF
LESSONS 16-20

FIND THE MISSING WORD

The sentences below are followed by a list of *italicized* words. For each sentence, write the word that fits best in the blank. Use each word only once. (The number in parentheses tells you the number of the story in which the word was first used.)

1. Every week .... come to our classroom to listen to the way Miss Colon teaches us in Spanish and in English.
2. We .... our bags in such a hurry that we left many things behind.
3. After breaking into the office, Sam .... all the papers that had his name on them.
4. I bought a bicycle to help me .... and lose weight.
5. Anyone who wants to .... must sit in the back part of the airplane.

144

6. Linda pulled on the cheap toy, and it came . . . . in her hands.

7. If you . . . . me when I am asleep, I wake up right away.

8. I didn't know how to play chess until my brother . . . . the game to me.

9. Your eyes can be . . . . if you read in a bad light.

10. One way to keep the . . . . in your body is to wear a hat.

(a) *apart* (16)   (f) *smoke* (17)
(b) *harmed* (19)   (g) *packed* (16)
(c) *exercise* (18)   (h) *heat* (20)
(d) *explained* (18) (i) *visitors* (20)
(e) *touch* (16)   (j) *destroyed* (17)

FINDING THE OPPOSITE

For each of the words in capitals, choose the word on the right that is most nearly opposite. (The number in parentheses tells you the number of the story in which the word was first used.)

1. DEAD (17)   (A) ugly (B) alive (C) still

2. GENTLE (19) (A) funny (B) kind (C) rough

3. APART (16)   (A) together (B) empty (C) straight

4. HARMED (19) (A) helped (B) hurt (C) shot

5. DAMAGED (19) (A) twisted (B) broke (C) fixed

6. MELTED (19) (A) frozen (B) creamed (C) lost

7. GRABBING (16)   (A) letting go (B) singing (C) fighting
8. GATHERED (20)   (A) folded (B) worked (C) sent away
9. HEAT (20)   (A) stove (B) cold (C) power
10. SHARING (20)   (A) keeping (B) giving away (C) telling

UNSCRAMBLING THE WORD

Each of the definitions below is followed by a scrambled word that fits the meaning. Unscramble the letters to find the word. The number in parentheses tells you the number of the story in which the word was first used.

1. part of the trunk of a fallen tree (16)   OLG

2. a flash of light in the sky (19)   GILTHGINN

3. filled with great surprise (18)   ZAMEDA

4. a small stream (16)   ECKER

5. very pleasing to taste (20)   LICEDSOUI

6. a thick growth of trees (17)   SOFTER

7. pulled (16)   GARDGED

8. brought about (17)   DESACU

9. measures of land (17)   SERAC

10. people who come to spend some time at a place (20)   TIVORSIS

146

FILL IN THE MISSING LETTERS

For each of the words below, write in the missing letters. (The number in parentheses tells you the number of the story in which the word was first used.) Use a separate sheet of paper.

1. s . . . . g (20)	dividing into parts
2. s . . . . . . l (18)	hard outer covering
3. a . . . . . t (17)	in pieces
4. c . . . . d (17)	made to happen
5. e . . . . d (18)	made clear
6. h . . . . . s (20)	places where bees live
7. h . . . . t (18)	to bring in the crops from the field
8. r . . . . s (18)	shakes; makes noise
9. p . . . . d (16)	filled up
10. s . . . . . e (16)	land near the water's edge

21. BE A CHEF!

WE'VE SEEN CONTESTS BETWEEN FOOTBALL TEAMS, FIGHTERS, AND WEIGHT LIFTERS.

BUT HAVE YOU EVER SEEN A COOKING CONTEST?

ST. PETERSBURG, Fla. — Six hundred student chefs * from all over the country were in the *contest*. Betty Ellison was in it, too, but she didn't think she had a *chance*. She was only in her first year of chef school. Still, her teachers told her to enter.

First, she entered the city contest here in St.

* Chef — the chief cook of a large cooking staff, as in a restaurant.

Petersburg. Everyone in the contest was given an *envelope* with *several recipes*. The recipes had to be changed into food within a given *period* of time. Betty Ellison won, with beef stroganoff **, chocolate cake, corn custard, and a palm tree of carrots and peppers.

This brought her to Fort Myers and the Florida *state* contest. "I was kind of nervous," Miss Ellison said later. "I burned two pans of peas . . . I don't know how I thought I could cook peas without water. But I didn't give up. I asked the *judge* if I might start again."

Her strawberry shortcake was just right. It saved the day. She won the state contest. Next, she was off to Birmingham, Alabama, for the country-wide contest. When her oven had *cooled,* she found herself tied for first place with a man who already made his living as a chef!

To break the tie, they both got a written cooking test. Miss Ellison missed two questions about things she hadn't yet been *taught* in class. She finished second, in all of the United States. Not bad for a person who was just learning to be a chef.

—ST. PETERSBURG TIMES

** Beef stroganoff — thinly cut beef served with mushrooms and sour cream.

CHECK YOUR UNDERSTANDING

1. Betty Ellison entered a contest for
   (A) eating
   (B) studying
   (C) cooking
2. Betty Ellison entered the contest because
   (A) she thought she would win
   (B) her teachers told her to
   (C) all the other students entered

3. Betty Ellison lost the
   (A) city contest
   (B) state contest
   (C) country-wide contest
4. Betty Ellison won the contest at Fort Myers because of her
   (A) strawberry shortcake
   (B) baked chicken
   (C) pans of peas
5. Which title tells most about the story?
   (A) She Didn't Think She Had a Chance to Win, But . . .
   (B) Contests in Florida
   (C) Written Tests Aren't Fair

FIND THE MISSING WORD

In your notebook, complete the following sentences with words from the story. You may look back at the story.

   1. Betty Ellison didn't think she had a . . . . . . to win.
   2. Everyone in the contest was given several . . . .
   3. She went to Fort Myers and the Florida . . . . contest.
   4. After she burned two pans of peas, she asked the . . . . if she might start again.
   5. She missed two questions about things she hadn't yet been . . . . in class.

FIRST THINGS FIRST

Arrange these events in the order in which they happened to Betty Ellison.

1. She won the contest at St. Petersburg.
2. She finished second because she missed two questions on a written cooking test.
3. She started chef school.
4. She burned two pans of peas.
5. She was tied for first with a man who made his living as a chef.

IMPROVING YOUR VOCABULARY

Choose the best word in Column B to complete each sentence in Column A. Use each word in Column B only once.

A	B
1. On a hot day, we . . . . off by swimming in the lake.	(a) several
2. The winner of the . . . . would get a record player.	(b) cooled
3. I put the letter into the . . . . and mailed it.	(c) envelope
4. I waited for only a short . . . . of time before Mr. Lee came out to talk to me.	(d) contest
5. Most people went home after the party, but . . . . . . of us stayed around to talk.	(e) period

---

SPELL IT RIGHT

In the last lesson, we learned about compound words. Which of these words is a compound word: *nervous* or *everyone*?

Some words cause spelling trouble because of

151

three letters in a row: *ght*. Look at the word *taught*. When you say the word, only the *t* of those three letters (*ght*) is sounded. The *g* and *h* are silent.

A. Copy each of these words. Then underline the *ght* at the end of each of them. Draw slanted lines through the *g* and *h* to show that they are not sounded. The first one is done for you.
    1. brought   brought
    2. thought
    3. right
    4. might
    3. sight

B. Write the word in each pair which is spelled right. Don't look back.
    1. rit, right
    2. sight, sigt
    3. brout, brought
    4. might, mit
    5. thought, thout

C. Fill in the missing letter in each word.
    1. thou . ht
    2. broug . t
    3. mi . ht
    4. sigh . .
    5. r . ght

D. One of these five words is spelled wrong. Pick out the wrong word and spell it right.

      sight   thouht   right   brought   might

EXPRESSING YOURSELF

1. Most family cooks are women while many of the great restaurant chefs are men. Why do you think this is so?

2. What skills does a person need to become a good cook?

3. Here is a recipe for Eggplant Fingers. You might want to express yourself by trying to make it.

2 one-pound egg plants   2 cups flour
2 cups milk   2½ cups bread crumbs
oil for deep frying   powdered sugar

Peel egg plants and cut into ½ inch strips, about 100. Heat oil in deep fat fryer to 375° F. Dip egg plant strips into milk, then into flour, into milk again, and then into the bread crumbs. Place about 12 at a time into a deep-fat frying basket and fry until golden brown, about 4 minutes. Place on paper towels. Add powdered sugar to the top of each strip.

4. One of Miss Ellison's winning meals was beef stroganoff, chocolate cake, corn custard, and a palm tree of carrots and peppers. Think of all your favorite foods and then list your ideas for "the perfect meal."

WRITE NOW!

Write a paragraph which starts with either of the following sentences:

One day it was up to me to cook dinner for the whole family.

or

I didn't give up.

22. THE AMERICAN BULLFIGHTER

PEOPLE IN MEXICO OR SPAIN SHOUT "OLÉ" WHEN A BULLFIGHTER MAKES A GOOD MOVE.

WAS THE "OLÉ" WORTH IT TO RAQUEL MARTINEZ?

One day when she was 17, Raquel Martinez went with her friends to a *bull* ring. It was in Mexico, just across from her home in San Diego, California. On a *dare* from her friends, the American entered the ring and *"fought"* a baby bull. "It was a *whole* new world," she remembers now.

Eight years and many bulls later, Martinez is now a *professional* bullfighter. She fought in small towns all over Mexico and has finally made it to Mexico City. From there, she wants to appear in the great bull rings of Spain and Latin America.

Martinez said that at first many bullfighters did not show *respect* for her because she was American, and a woman. They would play tricks on the bull so that it would make dangerous moves.

So far, she has *escaped* the horns of the bull. However, she has been *thrown* down and run over by bulls many times. She has been knocked *unconscious*. She has received a broken foot and a broken nose.

Martinez was asked if it's *worth* it. "Yes," she answered. "Some people want to be writers, actresses or doctors. I know I want to be a bullfighter."

— NEWSDAY (LONG ISLAND, N.Y.)

CHECK YOUR UNDERSTANDING

1. Raquel Martinez first fought a bull in
   (A) San Diego
   (B) Mexico
   (C) Spain
2. Other bullfighters caused trouble for Raquel Martinez by
   (A) pulling her cape
   (B) playing tricks on the bull
   (C) stealing her sword
3. Raquel Martinez has been hurt when bulls
   (A) bit her
   (B) fell on her
   (C) ran over her
4. How does Raquel Martinez feel about being a bullfighter?
   (A) Glad
   (B) Sorry
   (C) Afraid

5. Which title tells most about the story?
   (A) Spain and Latin America
   (B) Getting Help from Others
   (C) An Unusual Bullfighter

FIND THE MISSING WORD

In your notebook, complete the following sentences with words from the story. You may look back at the story.

   1. When she was 17, Raquel Martinez went with her friends to a . . . . ring.
   2. On a . . . . from her friends, the American entered the ring.
   3. At first Martinez did not have the . . . . of other bullfighters.
   4. She has been . . . . down and run over by bulls.
   5. She has been knocked . . . .

PROBABLY . . .

Choose the answer most likely to be true.

1. As a 17-year-old girl, Raquel Martinez was probably
   (A) lazy
   (B) shy
   (C) brave
2. When Raquel says at the end of the first paragraph, "It was a whole new world," she probably means that she
   (A) enjoyed fighting the baby bull
   (B) didn't like her friends anymore
   (C) liked Mexico better than San Diego

3. Most other bullfighters in Mexico are probably
   (A) American men
   (B) Mexican men
   (C) Mexican women
4. Mexico City is probably the place that has the greatest bull rings in
   (A) South America
   (B) the world
   (C) Mexico
5. At the time this story was written, Raquel was probably
   (A) 17 years old
   (B) 25 years old
   (C) 30 years old

IMPROVING YOUR VOCABULARY

Choose the best word in Column B to complete each sentence in Column A. Use each word in Column B only once.

A	**B**
1. Don was held prisoner, but he	(a) professional
2. The watch is . . . . $100.	(b) fought
3. Ali and Spinks . . . . for the heavyweight championship of the world.	(c) worth
	(d) escaped
4. She decided to make money from her hobby and became a	(e) whole
5. Read the . . . . book before you say whether or not you enjoyed it.	

SPELL IT RIGHT

In the last lesson, we learned how spelling trouble could come when *ght* ended a word. What letters are silent in the word *fight*?

There are other kinds of silent letters in words. Just like *ght,* these can also cause spelling trouble.

A. Copy each of these words. Then, draw a slanted line through the one silent letter in each word. The first one is done for you. Draw the line only through silent consonants.
1. writer   ⫽riter
2. whole
3. answer
4. would
5. knocked

B. Write the word in each pair which is spelled right. Don't look back.
1. anser, answer
2. nockd, knocked
3. writer, riter
4. whole, hol
5. would, woud

C. Fill in the missing letter in each word.
1. ans . . er
2. w . ole
3. wou . d
4. . . nocked
5. . . riter

D. One of these five words is spelled wrong. Pick out the wrong word and spell it right.

knocked   writer   would   whole   anser

158

EXPRESSING YOURSELF

1. Have you ever been asked, "What do you want to be when you grow up?" What might people say if you answered, "A bullfighter"? Why?
2. A bull might hurt a bullfighter with his horns but sooner or later the bull always loses. If that is the way all bullfights end, why do people go to see them?
3. How would you feel if a member of your family was a bullfighter? Would you want him or her to continue as a bullfighter?
4. List five other dangerous jobs at which people earn their living. Which of these jobs, if any, would you be willing to try? What would you like about that job?

WRITE NOW!

Write a paragraph using *one* of these topic sentences:

> *I'd rather not become a bullfighter.*
> *I know what it means to be afraid.*

23. THE NEWSPAPER CAME TOO LATE

READING CAN HELP A PERSON IN MANY WAYS.

COULD IT HELP SAVE LIVES?

RUDRAJ VILLAGE, India (UPI) — The newspaper was three days old. Kasu Reddi, a *post office* worker in India, was reading it. It was Saturday, a day off from work. Reddi started reading a story that said there was a *hurricane* heading for his village of Rudraj. Before he could finish the story, the hurricane struck.

As he was reading, his dog suddenly jumped up. The dog began barking wildly. Reddi heard *screams* and shouts from nearby homes. Then the terrible roar of the storm drowned out everything.

It took Reddi's mother just a few minutes to pack a few belongings. In that short time, *waist-*

deep water had *poured* into their small home. A tall tree in the backyard *crashed* onto the roof.

Reddi, his mother and the dog went for safety to the post office where he had worked for the past seven years. The post office is the strongest building in Rudraj.

"The coming of the hurricane sounded like a far-off roll of *drums* at first," Reddi said later. "When the full *force* of the storm struck, no one had time to stop and think. You did at the time whatever came first to your *mind*."

Rudraj was a village of about 2,000 people. "Now, after Saturday, only about 100 villagers are left *alive*. Maybe some are missing, or may have run away in a hurry, but most are dead, I know," Reddi said sadly.

"If only the newspaper had arrived sooner," he went on. "Who knows what might have been then?"

—DENVER POST

CHECK YOUR UNDERSTANDING

1. At the time the hurricane struck, Kasu Reddi was
   (A) playing with his dog
   (B) working in the post office
   (C) reading a newspaper
2. Reddi, his mother, and his dog went to the post office because it was
   (A) where they lived
   (B) the nearest building
   (C) the strongest building
3. After the hurricane, Reddi said that most of the villagers
   (A) were dead
   (B) had returned
   (C) were missing

4. The villagers might have been saved if
    (A) everyone had had a dog
    (B) the news of the hurricane had come sooner
    (C) there had been more boats
5. Which title tells most about the story?
    (A) A Terrible Hurricane
    (B) Reading Newspapers
    (C) A Man and His Dog

FIND THE MISSING WORD

In your notebook, complete the following sentences with words from the story. You may look back at the story.

1. Kasu Reddi is a . . . . worker.
2. He read that there was a . . . . heading for his Indian village.
3. . . . . -deep water had poured into their home.
4. The coming of the hurricane sounded like a far-off roll of . . . .
5. You did at the time whatever came first to your . . . .

FIRST THINGS FIRST

Arrange these events in the order in which they really happened.

1. The dog started barking wildly.
2. Only about 100 villagers were left alive.
3. Reddi's mother packed their belongings.
4. Reddi, his mother, and his dog went to the post office.
5. Reddi was reading a newspaper.

SIGHTS AND SOUNDS

The good reader "sees" what happens in a story and "hears" the sounds. Pick out the phrase in Column B that goes with the subject in Column A.

A	B
1. A tall tree in the backyard	(a) sounded like a far-off roll of drums.
2. The dog	(b) crashed onto the roof.
3. Waist-deep water	(c) began barking wildly.
4. The coming of the hurricane	(d) poured into their home.
5. The terrible roar of the storm	(e) drowned out everything.

IMPROVING YOUR VOCABULARY

Choose the best word in Column B to complete each sentence in Column A. Use each word in Column B only once.

A	B
1. The airplane . . . ., but luckily no one was hurt.	(a) screams
	(b) alive
2. We heard . . . . coming from the burning building.	(c) poured
	(d) force
3. The . . . . of the wind almost knocked Frank down to the ground.	(e) crashed
4. His car turned over twice, but Henry came out of it	
5. The rain . . . . down onto the roof of the house.	

163

SPELL IT RIGHT

We learned that you can tell the number of syllables in a word by counting the number of sounded vowels. How many syllables are there in *suddenly*?

A. Here are some three-syllable words found in the story. Copy the words and underline each vowel. You should have three vowels for each word. The first one is done for you.
  1. newspaper   newspaper
  2. terrible
  3. belonging
  4. whatever
  5. Saturday

B. Write the one word in each pair which is spelled right. Don't look back.
  1. watever, whatever
  2. newpaper, newspaper
  3. Saterday, Saturday
  4. terrable, terrible
  5. belonging, balonging

C. Fill in the missing letter in each word.
  1. Sat . .rday
  2. ne . .spaper
  3. w . .atever
  4. ter . .ible
  5. belongin . .

D. One of these five words is spelled wrong. Pick out the wrong word and spell it right.
belonging Saterday whatever newspaper terrible

164

EXPRESSING YOURSELF

1. Was it anyone's fault that most of the people in Kasu Reddi's village are no longer alive? If you had been the head of the village, what would you have done if you had learned about the coming hurricane?
2. Could this story have taken place in your town or city? Why?
3. Have you ever been in a hurricane or bad storm? Tell about it.
4. Talk with someone who works in your post office. Find out what his or her work is. Report back to the class with what you found out. Tell whether or not you would want a job in a post office.

WRITE NOW!

If you had only five minutes in which to leave your house because of fire, flood, or a hurricane, what things would you take with you? Make a list of five things you own which mean the most to you. Write a paragraph telling why these things are important to you.

24. STUDENT NURSES SAVE TRUCK DRIVER

WHEN HIS NEXT BIRTHDAY COMES AROUND, PAUL DAVIS WILL SEND FLOWERS TO SIX STUDENT NURSES.

HOW DID THEIR QUICK THINKING SAVE HIS LIFE?

WILLIAMSBURG, Ky. — Three weeks ago, Paul Davis was given up for dead. Today, the 24-year-old truck driver is on the road to getting well.

He might not be *except* for the quick work of six Cumberland College student *nurses*. They were traveling a few minutes behind his truck and got to him soon after it crashed.

The student nurses were on the way back from a day of training at an Oak Ridge hospital. When they saw the accident, they jumped out of their car. They were told that Davis was already dead, but they wouldn't move on without seeing for themselves. With the help of three men, they lifted him out. He was *bleeding* badly. One girl, Sandy Robinson, found an ice cream stick on the ground. She *wrapped* some gauze * around it and made an airway down his *throat*. Another student, Kathy Taylor, held his *tongue* down.

Then a third student, Sandy Brooks, found a *towel*. She *pressed* down with it on Davis' neck to slow the bleeding. A fourth student brought a *blanket* from their car and covered Davis. They kept his legs raised.

"We kept talking to him," Mrs. Taylor said. "We learned that the last thing you lose is your hearing."

The students kept Davis alive until he could be gotten to a hospital. There, he was brought out of danger. A doctor said that Davis would have *choked* to death if the girls had not used the ice cream stick to hold his tongue down. That, along with the other care given him by the six student nurses, is why he is alive today.

—LOUISVILLE COURIER-JOURNAL

* Gauze — a very thin, light cloth, easily seen through, often used for bandages.

CHECK YOUR UNDERSTANDING

1. After Paul Davis's truck crashed
   (A) it hit the car driven by the student nurses
   (B) people at the accident thought he was dead
   (C) he walked away from the truck without any help

167

2. Sandy Robinson helped Davis by
   (A) wrapping him with a towel
   (B) lifting Davis from the truck by herself
   (C) wrapping gauze around an ice cream stick

3. Sandy Brooks helped Davis by
   (A) holding Davis's tongue down
   (B) bringing a blanket from the car
   (C) pressing down with a towel on Davis's neck

4. A doctor said that by using the ice cream stick to keep Davis's tongue down, the student nurses
   (A) kept Davis from choking to death
   (B) gave Davis much needed food
   (C) hurt Davis

5. Which title tells most about the story?
   (A) Student Nurses Use What They Learn
   (B) The Dangers of Truck Driving
   (C) Never Believe What You're Told

FIND THE MISSING WORD

In your notebook, complete the following sentences with words from the story. You may look back at the story.

1. Paul Davis might not be alive . . . . for the quick work of six student nurses.
2. Sandy Robinson . . . . some gauze around an ice cream stick.
3. Kathy Taylor held his . . . . down.
4. Sandy Brooks found a . . . .
5. A doctor said that Davis would have . . . . . . to death.

168

FIRST THINGS FIRST

Arrange these events in the order in which they really happened.

1. The student nurses were told Davis was dead.
2. A doctor said Davis would have died if not for the care given him by the student nurses.
3. Davis was taken to a hospital.
4. Davis's truck overturned.
5. Sandy Robinson used an ice cream stick to make an airway down Davis's throat.

USING WHAT YOU LEARN

In nursing school, the students had learned what to do when caring for a person who has been in a serious accident. In Column A are listed five things they learned. In Column B are listed five things they did in caring for Paul Davis. Match what they learned to do in Column A with how they did it in Column B. For instance: 1.—(c).

A	**B**
1. Stop the bleeding	(a) They wrapped gauze around an ice cream stick
2. Keep the tongue down	(b) They covered Davis with a blanket
3. Keep the patient warm	(c) They pressed down with a towel on Davis's neck
4. Keep the blood going to the head	(d) They kept talking to Davis
5. Let the patient know that people are helping him	(e) They kept Davis's legs raised

Choose the best word in Column B to complete each sentence in Column A. Use each word in Column B only once.

A	**B**
1. While working, ... usually wear white uniforms.	(a) pressed
2. It was so cold, I had to sleep with an extra . . . . to keep warm.	(b) nurses
3. Phil was . . . . badly from the cut.	(c) throat
3. The doctor examined Nancy and said she had a sore . . . . and fever.	(d) blanket
5. Everyone was . . . . together in the crowded subway car.	(e) bleeding

SPELL IT RIGHT

Review of Words from Lessons 19-24

There is one word spelled wrong in each line. Pick out that word and spell it right.

1. anyone, writer, terible, whatever, became
2. whole, thought, bedroom, becaus, tore
3. threw, belonging, sight, Saterday, answer
4. said, right, left, nocked, might
5. brawt, would, outside, struck, newspaper

How many syllables are there in the word *traveling*?

To *spell it right,* we have to *say it right.* For example, *traveling* is often said as *trav-ling.* People who say it that way will often spell it wrong, leaving out the *e* between the *v* and the *l.*

A. Write the letter before the right way to say each of these words.

1. *already*   (a) AWL-REH-DEE
              (b) AW-RED-DEE
2. *towel*   (a) TOU-UL
              (b) TOE-EL
3. *seeing*   (a) SEE-UN
              (b) SEE-ING
4. *wouldn't*   (a) WUNT
              (b) WOOD-UNT
5. *minutes*   (a) MIN-ITS
              (b) MINTS

B. Write the word in each pair which is spelled right. Don't look back.

1. seein, seeing
2. minits, minutes
3. towel, towl
4. awready, already
5. woun't, wouldn't

C. Fill in the missing letter in each word.
1. wou . dn't
2. seein . .
3. tow . . l
4. a . . ready
5. min . . tes

D. One of these five words is spelled wrong. Pick out the wrong word and spell it right.
    awreddy   seeing   minutes   wouldn't   towel

EXPRESSING YOURSELF

1. A doctor said, "The first five minutes after someone is badly hurt are the most important minutes of his life." What did the doctor mean by that?
2. If the driver had been given up for dead, why did the nurses still try to save him? If you and five of your friends had been the first to reach the driver, what would you have done?
3. We are often told not to move a person who seems badly hurt. Why is that? When is it a good idea to move such a person?
4. Every weekend, hundreds of drivers get into bad accidents. List six rules which drivers should follow to keep from getting hurt. (Example: Don't drive too fast.)

WRITE NOW!

Make believe that you are the driver, Paul Davis. You are waking up in your hospital bed but cannot remember what happened to you. Write a paragraph or two about all the things that come into your mind as you are lying there.

25. THE MYSTERY BOOK THAT SAVED A CHILD

MYSTERY WRITERS SOLVE A LOT OF PUZZLES.

HOW COULD A MYSTERY BOOK SAVE A CHILD'S LIFE?

Nurse Martha Maitland sat next to the hospital bed of the *dying* child. The nurse looked sadly at the 19-month-old girl. The child had a strange *illness*. The best doctors in the world were unable to tell what her illness was.

Then the nurse returned to the *mystery* book she was reading. The book was *The Pale Horse*. It was written by Agatha Christie, the famous mystery writer. Nurse Maitland was nearly at the end of the book. The hero of the book was explaining how he had *discovered* the way the killings had been done.

The hero says in the book: "I read an *article* on thallium * poisoning. A lot of factory workers died, one after the other. No one knew what was causing the deaths. But one thing always happened to the one who died. His or her hair fell out."

Nurse Maitland put down her book and looked at the dying child. She began to think. The little girl had the same symptoms ** as the people who had been killed in Agatha Christie's book! She had high blood pressure.*** She had trouble *breathing*. She did not seem to hear when someone *spoke* to her. And, finally, her hair had started to fall out.

Nurse Maitland *hesitated*. Then she made up her mind and went to see the doctor. Everything else had been tried, so the nurse's idea was tested. She was right. Somehow, the child had taken into her body more than ten times the safe *amount* of the poison. Now the doctors knew what to do. They got *rid* of the thallium from the child's body. Soon, she was well enough to leave the hospital.

—NEWSDAY (LONG ISLAND, N.Y.)

* Thallium — an element used in some kinds of ant and rat poisons. Too much thallium in the human body can cause illness and even death.

** Symptoms — signs of one illness or another. For example, a certain kind of rash could be a symptom of measles.

*** Blood pressure — the pressure of the blood against the walls of the arteries.

CHECK YOUR UNDERSTANDING

1. The doctors of the 19-month-old girl

    (A) knew what her illness was, and could not cure her

(B) did not know what her illness was, and could not cure her

(C) knew what her illness was, and did not want to tell her

2. The factory workers who died from thallium poisoning were
   (A) in the hospital with the child
   (B) people who were killed in *The Pale Horse*
   (C) spoken about by the hero of *The Pale Horse*

3. After reading *The Pale Horse,* Nurse Maitland saw that
   (A) someone was trying to kill the little girl
   (B) the little girl had the same symptoms as the people mentioned in *The Pale Horse*
   (C) the little girl was getting better

4. The *best* clue Nurse Maitland had that the little girl had thallium poisoning was that the child's
   (A) hair had started to fall out
   (B) blood pressure was high
   (C) breathing was not regular

5. Which title tells most about the story?
   (A) Thallium Poisoning
   (B) The Mystery Book That Solved a Mystery
   (C) The Hard Life of a Nurse

FIND THE MISSING WORD

In your notebook, complete the following sentences with words from the story. You may look back at the story.

1. Nurse Martha Maitland sat next to the hospital bed of the . . . . child.

2. The child had a strange . . . . that caused her pain.

3. The hero had read an .... on thallium poisoning.

4. The child had trouble .... and was turning blue.

5. The doctors got .... of the thallium from the child's body.

FIRST THINGS FIRST

Arrange these events in the order in which they really happened.

1. Nurse Maitland read how the hero in *The Pale Horse* found out how the killings had been done.

2. The 19-month-old girl left the hospital.

3. The doctors couldn't tell what the child's illness was.

4. Nurse Maitland told the doctor she thought the child might have thallium poisoning.

5. Nurse Maitland saw that the child had the same symptoms as the people who had been killed in *The Pale Horse*.

WHAT'S THE REASON?

When you read, you sometimes have to be a good detective. You have to find out *why* things happen (just as Nurse Maitland did in this story). See if you can find the right "why" to answer each of these questions.

1. The workers in the factory died because
  (A) they had thallium poisoning
  (B) someone was trying to kill them
  (C) their hair fell out

2. Nurse Maitland thought that the dying child might have thallium poisoning because
  (A) the child had worked in a factory
  (B) the child had the same symptoms as the people mentioned in *The Pale Horse*
  (C) she was reading *The Pale Horse*
3. Nurse Maitland hesitated before going to the doctor because she
  (A) was afraid of him
  (B) would lose her job for reading mystery books
  (C) thought she might be mistaken
4. The little girl got well because
  (A) the doctors got rid of the thallium from her body
  (B) she now knew what was wrong with her
  (C) a new doctor took care of her

SPELL IT RIGHT

Final Review

There is one misspelled word in each line. Pick out that word and spell it right.

1. knocked, outside, perfict, dances
2. flowers, finaly, brought, writer
3. anser, right, rolled, left
4. pulling, says, newspaper, tryed
5. splashed, towel, geting, brave
6. allways, fires, I'd, police
7. home, inside, without, wasnt
8. parked, our, larg, maybe
9. angry, sayed, ground, letter
10. I'm, helping, chilren, asleep
11. mountins, pretty, safely, watched
12. whatever, money, driver, bushs

13. sigt, might, there, trouble
14. truely, summer, ever, friend
15. cooking, sounds, roared, somthing
16. teach, hous, going, made
17. corner, hotest, hills, struck
18. Saterday, really, threw, around
19. alreddy, life, started, clothes
20. runing, stomach, too, wouldn't
21. bedroom, can't, becaus, working
22. thought, begins, anyone, thrugh
23. sudenly, young, trees, became
24. write, terible, would, shook
25. break, walking, whol, country

IMPROVING YOUR VOCABULARY

Choose the best word in Column B to complete each sentence in Column A. Use each word in Column B only once.

A	**B**
1. It's a .... to me how Jenny passed that hard math test without even studying.	(a) spoke
	(b) amount
	(c) hesitated
	(d) discovered
2. The recipe for the cake calls for a small .... of nuts.	(e) mystery
3. The coach .... to Len about being late to practice, but it didn't do any good.	
4. Anna .... before telling Pat she would join her club.	
5. Charles has .... a new drink—water!	

EXPRESSING YOURSELF

1. Pretend that you are a doctor. Make up five questions that you might ask a person who has bad headaches.
2. Have you ever been in a hospital or been treated by a doctor? Tell about it.
3. Do you know how to treat someone who might have been poisoned? If you were baby-sitting, what would you do for a child who ate aspirins thinking they were candy? What would you do if a child drank some household cleaner by mistake?
4. Have you ever read a mystery book or seen a mystery at the movies or on TV? What things make a mystery fun to read or see?
5. There are many TV programs which show doctors and nurses at work. Do you watch any of these programs? Why do you think people like to watch them?

WRITE NOW!

Here is the first sentence of a story:

The doctors did not know what was wrong with me.

In a paragraph or two, finish the story.

REVIEW OF
LESSONS 21-25

FINDING THE MISSING WORD

The sentences below are followed by a list of italicized words. For each sentence, write the word that fits best in the blank. Use each word only once. (The number in parentheses tells you the number of the story in which the word was first used.)

1. She made $20,000 as a . . . . bullfighter.
2. Although we . . . . hard, we lost the game anyway.
3. The police had to use . . . . to break the door down.
4. Everyone came to the party . . . . Sam and Ellis.

180

5. Edith sent me . . . . letters, but I never wrote to her.

6. After his . . . . , Martin had to take a long rest in the country.

7. You will find your . . . . on the sink in the bathroom.

8. Rita's dress cost $100, but she thought it was . . . . it.

9. One of the chef's best . . . . is for apple pie.

10. Sally put the new belt around my . . . . to see if it would fit.

(a) *illness* (25) (f) *worth* (22)
(b) *professional* (22) (g) *towel* (24)
(c) *waist* (23) (h) *fought* (22)
(d) *force* (23) (i) *except* (24)
(e) *recipes* (21) (j) *several* (21)

FINDING THE OPPOSITE

For each of the words in capital letters, choose the word on the right that is most nearly OPPOSITE. (The number in parentheses tells you the number of the story in which the word was first used.)

1. TAUGHT (21) (A) learned (B) lost (C) held

2. SPOKE (25) (A) told (B) listened (C) played

3. ALIVE (23) (A) dead (B) well (C) safe

4. COOLED (21) (A) froze (B) heated (C) passed

5. THROWN (22) (A) fell (B) caught (C) seat

6. WHOLE (22) (A) pit (B) part (C) rim

7. DISCOV-   (A) land (B) hunted (C)
   ERED (25)   lost
8. UNCON-   (A) awake (B) smart (C)
   SCIOUS (22)   dumb
9. ESCAPED (22)   (A) ran (B) was caught
        (C) stopped
10. PROFES-   (A) teacher (B) amateur
    SIONAL (22)   (C) worker

UNSCRAMBLING THE WORD

Each of the definitions in Column A below is followed, in Column B, by a scrambled word that fits the meaning. Unscramble the letters to find the word. (The number in parentheses tells you the number of the story in which the word was first used.)

A	**B**
1. said	POSEK (25)
2. number	NATOUM (25)
3. something we cannot understand	TYMREYS (25)
4. stopped before going on	SHEDITETA (25)
5. covered	RAWPDEP (24)
6. honor	SETRPCE (22)
7. loud shouts	MESCRAS (23)
8. a game or a race	TOSNECT (21)
9. person who listens to both sides in court	DUJEG (21)
10. pushed against	DESPRES (24)

FILL IN THE MISSING LETTERS

Each of the words in Column A has letters missing. Write in the missing letters. A definition for each word is given in Column B. (The number in parentheses tells you the number of the story in which the word was first used.)

A

1. h . . . . e (23)
2. i . . . . s (25)
3. t . . . . e (24)
4. p . . . . d (23)
5. r . . . . t (22)
6. t . . . . t (21)
7. b . . . . g (24)
8. n . . . . s (24)
9. d . . . . d (25)
10. u . . . . s (22)

B

1. a big storm
2. sickness
3. part of your mouth
4. rained hard
5. admire and honor
6. gave lessons to
7. losing blood
8. they take care of the sick
9. found
10. in a deep sleep

ACKNOWLEDGMENTS

For permission to reprint and adapt copyrighted materials, grateful acknowledgment is made to the following publishers and news services:

"Round and Round" reprinted with permission of *United Press International*.

"A Day in the Life of a Russian Runner" reprinted with permission from the *Miami Herald*.

"The Kids Don't Bother Charlie" copyright © *Newsday*, Inc. Reprinted by permission.

"The Football Player" reprinted with permission of *United Press International*.

"The Hot Wheels Kid" reprinted with permission of *The Denver Post*.

"Bulletproof Vest" reprinted with permission of the *Chicago Sun Times*.

"A 73-Year-Old High Diver" Copyright, 1977, *Los Angeles Times*. Reprinted by permission.

"Dumb Bank Robber" Copyright 1977 *New York News Inc.* Reprinted by permission.

"The Biter" reprinted with permission of Ann Landers, Field Newspaper Syndicate and the *Washington Post*.

"Hero Forgot to Tell Mom" reprinted with permission from *The Miami Herald*.

"Teen Model Says It's Hard Work" reprinted with permission of the *Bellmore Life*.

"Mr. Kool" © 1972 by The New York Times Company. Reprinted by permission.

"From Cop to Doc" © 1972 by The New York Times Company. Reprinted by permission.

"All-Around Actress" reprinted with permission of *The Milwaukee Journal*.

"Dog Rescues Master from Creek" reprinted with permission of *The Courier-Journal*.

"Blackened Land Gets New Life" reprinted with permission of *The Milwaukee Journal*.

"Mexican Jumping Beans" from "Living High on Beans" by Charles Hillinger. Copyright, 1972, Los Angeles Times. Reprinted by permission.

"Lightning Man" reprinted with permission of The Associated Press.

"Bees in the Bedroom Wall" reprinted with permission of the *Staten Island Advance*.

"Be a Chef!" reprinted with permission of the *St. Petersburg Times*.

"The American Bullfighter" Copyright Newsday, Inc. Reprinted by permission.

"The Newspaper Came too Late" reprinted with permission of *United Press International*.

"Student Nurses Save Truck Driver" reprinted with permission of *The Louisville Courier-Journal*.

"The Mystery Book That Saved a Child" Copyright Newsday, Inc. Reprinted by permission.